God and the Gangs

D1589851

Also by Robert Beckford

God of the Rahtid
Jesus is Dread
Dread and Pentecostal

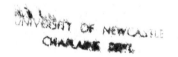

God and the Gangs

An Urban Toolkit for Those Who Won't
Be Sold Out, Bought Out or Scared Out

ROBERT BECKFORD

DARTON·LONGMAN + TODD

First published in 2004 by
Darton, Longman and Todd Ltd
1 Spencer Court
140–142 Wandsworth High Street
London SW18 4JJ

Unless otherwise indicated, scripture quotations are taken from the Revised
Standard Version, © 1946, 1952 the Division of Christian Education of the
National Council of the Churches of Christ in the United States of America.

ISBN 0 232 52518 8

A catalogue record for this book is available from the British Library.

Phototypeset by Intype Libra Ltd, London
Printed and bound in Great Britain by
Page Bros, Norwich, Norfolk

To Professor Randall Bailey,
scholar, friend and mentor

Contents

Foreword

Little more than two weeks after the brutal murders of Charlene Ellis and Latisha Shakespeare I was one of many who took part in a community event at the ground of Aston Villa Football Club. The title of the event made its intention clear: 'Youth Cry Life not Death – Enough is Enough'. The event was organised by the community for the community – it was the first public response of a community in shock at the loss of two of its daughters. It was also a wake up call to wider society to think seriously about the issues of gang violence and gun crime.

In writing this book Robert Beckford looks beyond the headlines that brought the community of Aston into the media spotlight and considers how we might understand the issues of education, employment, culture and social change that affect and influence us all as a society. He also provides a theological toolkit for reflection on these issues as well as providing practical suggestions on how each of us can contribute to the changes that need to be brought about in our communities.

For those unfamiliar with theological reflection, this book offers a good place to start. For those familiar with theological thought, this book challenges the need for reflection to be carried out in the context of the world around us, evoking the role of the radical Jesus of Nazareth in transforming the society in which he lived.

Mahatma Gandhi wrote that the challenge for each of us is to become the change that we want to see in our society. *God and the Gangs* is a serious and meaningful contribution to achieving that change.

Robert Beckford's book is essential reading on a disturbing topic which most of us acknowledge but with which few of us know how to deal. A bold and angry challenge to a community which has come to accept the inhuman consequences of individualism – always looking the other way.

+ **John Sentamu**

Acknowledgements

While the opinions and ideas within this book are my own, several people have contributed to its production. First, I would like to thank the MA and MPhil students in Black Theology at the University of Birmingham for their feedback and comments on the text. Pastors Kate Coleman and Cham Kaur-Mann and the congregation at the Regeneration Centre in Birmingham were always helpful. Dr Lurleen Willis provided some important comments and corrections for which I am truly grateful. Finally, my sisters and parents have continued to make my work possible by supporting me and my family. Last and by no means least, I want to 'hail up' my wife Charlie and son Micah for their unwavering love which makes life worthwhile.

This book is dedicated to my mentor and friend, Professor Randall Bailey, who has intervened at key moments in my academic career to keep me on track and focused.

Introduction

Sold Out, Bought Out, Scared Out

Two Teenagers Shot Dead in Birmingham

Two teenagers were shot dead early this morning after a dispute at a party in Birmingham. Police said a member of the public heard a 'considerable' number of shots shortly after 4 a.m. from the hairdressing salon where the party was held.

On arrival officers found a 17-year-old girl and 18-year-old woman and a third teenager with gunshot wounds outside at the back of the premises in Birchfield Road, Aston.

The 17- and 18-year-old died of their wounds despite efforts by the police and paramedics to revive them while the third was taken to hospital, where her injuries are not thought to be life-threatening.

It later emerged that a fourth teenager at the party was admitted to hospital with gunshot wounds.

The road around the murder scene was sealed off while officers conducted house-to house-inquiries. A car riddled with bullet holes was later recovered nearby and is being forensically examined but police do not know how it was linked to the killings.

Guardian
2 January 2003

When two teenagers, Charlene Ellis and Latisha Shakespeare, were gunned down for no apparent reason in the early hours of 2 January 2003, Birmingham was in shock. The two girls were out celebrating at a new year party when they were caught in the crossfire between two rival gangs in the Aston region of Birmingham. Sadly, despite numerous witnesses being present at the scene, it took ten months for several to come forward and on 13 November 2003 the police made their first significant arrests.

Encouragingly, black majority churches, or what I will refer to throughout as urban churches[1] responded swiftly to the shootings by organising community meetings to enable people to express their feelings and explore ways forward for the community. The most public outcome was an anti-gun rally organised mostly by young black women. Eight thousand people attended the event at Aston Villa Football Club a few weeks later to hear black musicians, rappers and members of the families of the deceased call for an end to gun crime and gang violence in the city and nation.

Gun crime in Britain is on the rise. Home Office figures show nearly 10,000 incidents involving firearms in England and Wales in 2002/2003, including a record 97 murders, with a further 558 serious casualties, representing a 35 per cent increase on the previous year. Gun crime has risen steadily for the last four years. In 2000/2001, the increase was driven by a 46 per cent surge in the use of illegal handguns, which the media and police claim are seen as a fashion accessory by some in the inner cities. Guns are now used in 70 per cent of all robberies in England and Wales.[2]

Several meetings were held throughout February and March 2003 to determine a meaningful response from the churches and community to the shootings. The result has been a renewed effort by urban church leaders to work together with community activists in addressing the problems associated with lateral violence (so-called black-on-black violence) in urban communities.

Despite being very good at being shocked, urban churches have not been at the forefront of deciphering the underlying causes of their shock. Ironically, many secular activists view the urban Church as historically ineffective in challenging moral and social decay in the inner city, even though the vast majority of these congregations are located at the heart of communities experiencing increased levels of crime, gun violence, the menace of crack cocaine, and sophisticated forms of racialised exclusion.

To respond effectively there is a need for new insight and practice by urban churches. As a participant and observer of the churches' engagement with the community during the first few months after the shootings, I noted limited theological, cultural and social frameworks being used to make sense of the crisis. A defining moment for me was when at one of the meetings a black church leader received rapturous applause for stating that 'no handcuffs could be put around Satan and the task of the churches in the face of gun violence [was] to pray!' Decades of anti-intellectualism in some sectors of the African Caribbean urban Church have made it increasingly difficult to address complex social issues without reducing the matter to a call for prayer. Just as disturbing was the demographic representation at the meetings. There were never more than one or two black men under the age of 30 present at any of the meetings I attended. This suggests that the most basic task of listening to young blacks was not under serious consideration.

The motivation for writing this book was born out of the need to offer alternative ways of analysing and reflecting on what is taking place from the vantage point of urban churches. I am not neglecting or dismissing the need to pray and seek spiritual guidance, but I believe that spiritual guidance does not exclude serving God with our minds by exploring the intellectual dimensions of the problem. This text aims to provide social, cultural, political and theological resources for those within urban churches searching for new tools to combat the oppression of gun crime and gang violence in our midst.[3]

It is my intention that this book will be read by groups and individuals seeking new insights and practices. To this end each chapter concludes with a series of questions for discussion on the subject at hand and its practical implications. While the focus is on Birmingham, the widespread nature of gun crime and gang violence across urban Britain broadens the audience and implications of this work.

Gang Structure, Crime and Race

Gangs in a variety of forms have always been a part of the urban landscape. Peer gangs have been a part of the African Caribbean community for most of my 38 years. My now retired 70-year-old father was part of a group of 'rudies' (Jamaican rude boys) in the Midlands area during the early 1960s. His group of friends 'moved together' (hung out) at parties, clubs and other social venues. Amongst second-generation African Caribbean youths, posses, crews, brethren and peeps are some of the names given to cliques of men and women who form a social group based on friendship, locality or family ties. However, what appears to have made gangs problematic is the association with drug-centred criminal activity and the increased use of firearms. These associations at the heart of urban youth culture are being utilised for more sinister purposes. So how do we define a gang?

According to research conducted in Nottingham in 2003, gangs operate on at least three levels. At the top are economic gangs. These are 'very professional and are behind major drug smuggling crimes'. Their aim is to make vast sums of money and they will use tremendous violence to protect their markets. They have a hierarchy and structure comparable with that found in legitimate businesses. For instance, 'good' workers are promoted to more responsible positions in the gang.

In the middle are precursory gangs. These are peer group gangs which evolve over time so that 'some of their activities echo the structure and scale witnessed in economic gangs'. However, precursory gangs commit lesser offences such as small-time drug dealing, theft and burglary. At the bottom of the structure are peer gangs. These are loose co-operatives of youths 'united by friendship, family or geographical affiliation'. They are not involved in major crime or violence but many commit nuisance offences.[4]

There has always been a strong relationship between race and crime in the context of postwar Britain. Put simply, offences committed by black people are viewed as more problematic than similar offences committed by white people.[5] So when discussing gang activity we must be aware that black gangs will always be perceived by the media, the police and the Government as more dangerous than their white counterparts.

There are a variety of explanations for the rise in gun-gang activity in urban areas. Naturally, greater availability of guns has played a significant role in the increase in gun crime. However, I want to place this phenomenon within recent postwar political and social history. I believe that the underlying causes of gun crime and gang violence are the product of a systemic failure, or multiple breakdown, in social, cultural, political, communal and moral forces in the urban context. This perception is supported by recent research which claims that: 'deprivation and a lack of adequate support from statutory agencies, including schools, are other prime factors'.[6]

My perception is also based on personal experience. In 2001, I spent a year working with both young and adult offenders within the prison system. One of the most striking aspects of their lives was the number of structures and institutions that had failed to curb their criminal behaviour. In most cases these failures were multiple; family, schools, voluntary organisations and social welfare had all failed at the same time. Identifying systemic failure does not mean that we ignore personal responsibility. Young people committing crimes have to be held accountable for their actions. There is no justifiable reason for condoning drug dealing and the use of weapons However, it remains essential that we address the systemic failure which shows itself in structural breakdown within families, the law, education and employment.

Gun crime and gang violence is made in urban Britain. It is the product of over a decade of failed education, welfare and employment policies. Many of the black youths involved in gun crime were born and raised during the Conservative reign of the 1980s. They are Margaret Thatcher's grandchildren, warehoused in substandard schools, ignored in underfunded communities and sent to young offenders' institutions and prisons in disproportionate numbers. We are reaping a grim harvest from the brutal assault on urban social amenities, family structures and employment possibilities in the 1980s and early 1990s. The rise of a multi-million pound crack cocaine industry in the midst of urban decay has merely exploited a frustrated army of the disaffected and socially excluded.

Systemic failure has moral and ethical consequences. I believe that for some time we have been witnessing a form of outlaw culture amongst groups of our young people. Faced with an inability to create a meaningful place in the world, many have simply opted out of mainstream life, choosing alternative economic and social existences.

How do churches ministering to these communities approach these issues? More specifically, what does God have to say to the gangs? Historically, the Church has responded to this question in at least three different ways.[7]

Firstly, there is the withdrawal response. Here, the Church sidesteps gun crime and gang violence and focuses on the world to come, preparing for life with Jesus in heaven through devotion to the spiritual life. To this end, believers are encouraged to be hard-working, morally upright and socially passive. Consequently, while church members may flourish, the world outside the Church and issues such as social decay and political upheaval are not given the same attention or importance as the life of the church. For this camp, 'the poor will always be with us' and the Church cannot solve every social problem. This does not mean that the Church completely ignores social issues; when crises arise, their main response is to pray, inviting divine presence and power into situations. For those with this perspective, it is only the Spirit of God that can change the way things are.

Secondly, there is the project-work response. Here the task of the Church is to do good works in order to help those caught up in gun crime and gang violence. Guided by prayer and the witness of the Spirit, the Church is to be a beacon for all in need, providing welfare to the community. So churches run youth clubs for people at risk, day care centres and training courses for the unemployed. By practising the unconditional love of God the Church functions as a healing balm within the community. Its love 'casts out all fears' (1 John 4:18). Within this perspective, we prepare for the life to come by not only by developing individual spirituality (withdrawal) but also by devotion to those whom Jesus defines as 'the least of these' (Matthew 25:40).

A third response is to struggle for peace and justice and an end to gun crime and negative gang cultures. The prophetic emphasis of the Gospel inspires this perspective. The prophetic task is to provide a vision of the way that things should be and the means by which peace and justice can be achieved. While affirming the importance of good works as a source of healing, this approach recognises that Jesus' example encourages us to confront the unjust forces responsible for causing distress.

Through his nonviolent confrontation of legal, religious and social structures that oppressed, marginalised and demeaned, Jesus heralded an alternative value system and social order. It was so radical that it provoked the authorities to conspire to get rid of him. For Jesus, those outside the community, the outcasts of his time, were made central to God's redemptive plan. The prostitute, the tax collector, the revellers, the Samaritans and the sick were invited to be part of the Kingdom of God (Luke 6:20–26). For the prophetic model, the Church's task requires a radical commitment to the oppressed of our time. In the urban context the failing schoolchild, the disaffected youth, the drug user and the abused teenager become central to the prophetic mission.

However, the prophetic approach also sounds a note of caution, as to struggle for a social climate free of domination in today's world is dangerous and will get people into trouble. Confronting the forces of evil in the world never goes unchallenged, and no matter what level of resistance you are engaged in, there are forces of non-being (evil) out there to get you! Black theologian James Cone states that the measure of a good and committed Christian is the amount of trouble they find themselves in with authorities that oppress people.

This book is grounded in the third approach outlined above. I believe that the urban Church must be prophetic in its ministry towards gang members in particular and disaffected youths in general. I believe that the prophetic approach is the only viable way of creating a countercultural, politically engaged and self-sacrificing worshipping community able to transform and empower the disaffected and marginalised in urban Britain. The withdrawal and project-work approaches are far too limited to intervene meaningfully and to challenge the outlaw culture which seeks to steal, kill and destroy without conscience or impunity. Later in this book, I will describe the contours of prophetic action, but for now I want to address the obstacles that prevent the urban Church from fulfilling this task.

Sold Out

One of the major dangers facing urban churches anxious to live out the prophetic mandate is selling out or compromising to the values of the world system. 'Sold out' refers to pastors and churches who crave power, status and material wealth. Often this lust is justified as a divinely appointed opportunity to influence the community or city. However, in real terms, selling out is nothing short of exchanging the radical, sacrificial and demanding aspects of the Gospel for a luxurious lifestyle. The growth of prosperity doctrines and positive confession techniques in urban churches are a few contemporary symptoms of this malaise.[8]

In 1 Corinthians 1:26–28, the Apostle Paul reminds the Corinthians that they don't need to sell out or succumb to the values of the world system, and in particular to the idea that the Church competes in the world by means of worldly power status and wealth:

> For consider your call, brethren; not many of you were wise according to worldly standards, not many were powerful, not many were of noble birth; but God chose what is foolish in the world to shame the wise, God chose what is weak in the world to shame the strong, God chose what is low and despised in the world, even things that are not, to bring to nothing things that are, so that no human being might boast in the presence of God.

What I am trying to get at here is that there are pastors and churches that have ignored the countercultural value system of the Christian faith. This does *not* mean that we should stop striving to be successful, but that urban churches should promote an alternative way of thinking and being in order to 'achieve' in a radically different way, with values based on the model that Jesus lays down for believers. When a church is sold out, it has no viable alternatives to offer. It becomes just another 'gang' competing for turf and resources in the community.

Bought Out

A church that sells out is easily 'bought out'. Whereas selling out concerns values, the danger of being bought out is in unscrupulous alliances. A local black politician told me that one of the reasons why certain church leaders were not available when needed to publicly criticise the police and local authority during recent unrest was because they and their church projects were on the payroll and received funding from those organisations. While there is nothing wrong with accepting funding from legitimate sources, there is a problem when sources of revenue or support are seen as more important than defending the weak or standing for justice. Often there is simply a lack of discernment or a failure to think through the consequences of receiving funding. To avoid becoming a lukewarm presence in the community, the urban Church must guard against being seduced by the benefits gained from these associations. It needs to be a living and committed presence in the community, unafraid of taking on any manifestation of evil or injustice, even if it means risking funding or support.

Scared Out

The third danger is that church members give up, and move out and avoid confronting criminals in the community. Many black Christians have been 'scared out' of living or serving in the most deprived parts of the inner city. I admit that there are times when this has been a real issue for me. I lived for ten years opposite a bail hostel in Handsworth, Birmingham. I chose to live in that area despite being able to afford to live in a more upwardly mobile suburb. I was scared out by what I perceived as a lack of meaningful policing and a feeling of being endangered by criminal activity.

I found it amazing that people on my street could name the location and working hours of a host of crack houses, drug dens and illegal gambling halls, while the police appeared to be oblivious to their existence. I often wondered if the inability of the police to close down, raid or challenge these places of criminal activity was due to their being comfortable with these criminal locations being 'contained' in a black neighbourhood. The question of inadvertent police collusion with criminal activity in Birmingham's inner city was raised during several of the public meetings held after the shootings of Charlene Ellis and Latisha Shakespeare. For me, the fear of policing by containment was as great as the fear of crime itself.

I was also scared out of parts of the inner city because of the fear of criminals. A defining moment for me was on one summer's day in 2000 when I saw a young neighbour of mine carrying a handgun; I was too afraid confront him or inform the police. A few months later, when I was speaking at a local young offenders' institution, I saw the same youth there on a charge of attempted murder. In that moment I realised that I did not have the courage to do the right thing; I was too scared.

Tragically, being scared out is often justified theologically. Some argue that the urban context is irredeemable and, like the disciples, want to call down fire from heaven to destroy wickedness (Luke 9:54) rather than seek to save.

We should note that being scared out is bound up with the last hundred years of urban Church history. There is a long tradition in Britain of the Church escaping the troubles of the urban context and finding solace in the suburbs.[9] Even within the churches that have stayed put, there still exists the danger of making the Church a social escalator, consciously moving members up the ladder to flee the perils of the neighbourhood.

The option of flight from the inner city now confronts many African and African Caribbean congregations. In the postwar, postcolonial climate, black migrants were forced into the worst housing and neighbourhoods of most major cities.[10] Consequently the first black congregations emerged in the inner ring. Today, these congregations are strategically placed to be at the forefront of the battle against rising crime, violence and poverty, as long as they are willing to hold their ground and keep the faith.

God and the Gangs

How do urban churches avoid being sold out, bought out or scared out? In this book I want to offer a selection of tools to combat this triple failing. Every handyperson knows that tools never do the work for you; you still have to engage with the matter at hand and do the work. So the tools presented here are for readers to use and experiment with. In every toolkit there exists a selection of implements to help you get a job done. This selection is limited and not able to offer help with every task. This toolkit is designed to make sense of gun crime and gang violence and the tools are chosen and shaped to reflect particular theological presuppositions.

As I have argued elsewhere,[11] I believe that the political struggle for justice among marginalised people and groups is often fought in part in the realm of culture. For some time now cultural theorists such as Paul Gilroy and Lola Young,[12] have argued that what we see, hear and consume has a powerful influence on public opinion, economic forces and social attitudes. One way in which urban churches can engage in this struggle (the politics of representation) is to learn how to deconstruct and make sense of what we see, hear and feel. We will be better equipped to affirm, rebuke and challenge from an informed position.

This book has four sections, all of which are related parts of a process of interpreting and acting. The first section concerns the *method* and perspectives that inform and shape this approach. The first chapter addresses the need to do theology in a new way which responds to the current crisis. It proposes a four-part process of making sense of the way things are, namely *experience, analysis, biblical reflection and interpretation* and *action*. These categories shape the book. The second chapter in this section explores the importance of experience and context, in particular why we need to respond to systemic failure in our theological enterprise.

The second section is *analytical*. It provides a selection of tools for understanding aspects of the urban context. Urban churches often avoid serious analysis. For instance, when I was growing up in the Wesleyan Holiness Church in Britain, I was taught to interpret the Bible without considering the social world in which I lived. Consequently, I approached the Scriptures only with personal questions, rather than being informed by the social, cultural and economic issues that surrounded me.

This section offers an alternative approach that takes social analysis seriously. As mentioned above, a religious–cultural lens informs my perspective on the urban context, and the tools that I offer are related to this standpoint. I offer four broad analytical frameworks. These are *postcolonialism, cultural analysis, Afrocentrism* and *critical whiteness*. It is not possible in a text of this size to describe the minute details of each framework; my aim is to provide a general idea of where each approach leads. My hope is that those reading this book will be inspired to explore the specific political, economic and cultural ramifications of the analytical tools on offer.

This second section begins with a chapter on *postcolonialism*. This is a complex discipline that attempts to identify how values and traditions from the colonial era have been reworked and reused in postcolonial contexts such as urban Britain. Images of dangerous black men who must be controlled as well as the internalisation of racism by black people have their roots in the racialising processes forged in the colonial era. Why postcolonial analysis? Because of its appreciation of how the past has an impact, both historically and politically, on our perception of the present crisis.

The fourth chapter explores *culture*. Understanding culture is important because of the alleged causal relationship between hip-hop cultures, gun crime and gang violence. As will be shown in the chapter, there is a belief that hip-hop is to blame for young black men choosing to bear arms. By examining the complexity of urban culture, the chapter seeks to explore how expressive cultures are forms of resistance and celebration as well as scapegoats for urban ills.

The fifth chapter examines *Afrocentrism*, a way of exploring blackness which takes black history, politics and identity seriously. Holding common ground and differences in tension, this chapter describes Afrocentricity and assesses the meaning and significance of identity politics in the urban context, showing how poor black self-image and limited awareness of black history and culture can contribute to gun crime and gang violence.

The sixth chapter and final tool that I offer in this section is *critical whiteness*. To make sense of systemic failure we must also explore the role of ethnicity and power in the urban context. Systemic failure is not just a 'black thing'; it is also related to the actions of white people and white urban communities. While a great deal of time and attention have been spent on exploring the notion of being black, few theological explorations examine how whiteness is constructed and its relationship to privilege. Often, in our attempt to dialogue with urban youth, we forget the need to address the ways in which a negative and unreformed whiteness affects the opportunities and resources available to young blacks in the urban arena.

The third section explores *biblical reflection*. To summarise, it looks at how the social analysis of experience enables a more focused examination of the cultural and political themes within the biblical text. As mentioned earlier, without meaningful exploration of our social context we limit what we can extrapolate from Scripture. The seventh chapter details the business of interpreting Scripture, that is, *biblical hermeneutics*. This brief introduction examines the nuts and bolts of interpretation, namely, the forces and institutions that have an impact on interpretation and the places in which meaning occurs.

The eight and ninth chapters provide two hermeneutical approaches to the biblical text that offer a radical and political framework for interpreting the social world. These are *reader response*, and *ideological interpretation*. Reader response looks at how readers interpret the Bible. Here it is argued that if we bring to the fore our cultural and political themes, we can facilitate a reading of Scripture that more readily engages with the pressing cultural and political concerns of the urban context. The second approach, ideological interpretation, focuses on issues of power in the life of the reader and in the life of the text. By recognising both approaches, we can better address the controlling themes in urban interpretation.

To illustrate these hermeneutical issues, the final chapter in this section, chapter 10, is a case study of how the Bible can be reread through reader response and ideological criticism. In the form of a sermon entitled, 'Doing Wrong to Make Right: A rereading of Exodus 1:15–21' I examine how issues of race, justice and violence in the text have an impact on our present situation.

The final section concerns how we act in response to experience, analysis and reflection. Chapter 11 presents *prophetic action* as a legitimate response to systemic failure. The aim is to place within a broader context the response of community initiatives such as Street Pastors in Brixton, Young Disciples Youth Development in Birmingham and Mothers Against Guns. All of these projects attempt to engage with contemporary gun crime issues based on a particular understanding. Some believe in intervention, others in protesting to the police and national government. Through a critical dialogue with the urban toolkit it is hoped that new insights and ideas for practice will be offered to these groups.

SECTION 1

Methodology

Chapter 1

Urban Style

Towards a Relevant Theological Method

In this first section we will explore theological method. We begin with method because I believe that our approach to theology, or putting into expression the meaning of God in the world, will determine our interpretation. Conservative men and women tend to produce conservative theology. Bigots tend to produce theological ideas infected by discrimination. I want to outline a theological method that will more effectively address the social problems related to gun crime and gang violence.

This section has two chapters. The first explores the hermeneutical spiral as a way of doing theology, and the second examines the role of personal and communal experience as a legitimate starting-point for exploring and participating in what God is doing in the world today. I begin with the hermeneutical spiral.

The word 'theology' worries a lot of people. Mainstream publishers dislike it because they think it's a commercially unattractive term. In the black urban Church it is viewed as a form of kryptonite, removing the 'real faith' of believers.[1] Why is this the case in urban churches? There are a number of reasons and here I will discuss two of them.

Firstly, academic theology and talk of theological method is still regarded as the preserve of liberal, out of touch and boring ivory/ebony tower scholars. There is some truth in this statement. For far too long critical thinking in the theological academy has been distanced from the real-life experience and concerns of everyday church folk. This has been particularly true in the case of black African Caribbean Christian concerns. More academic books have been written in Britain in the last fifty years on being nice to animals (animal theology) than on dealing with racial discrimination. Even the growth and contribution of black Christianity in Britain has been ignored by the white theological academy. This speaks volumes to black folk about how little scholarly attention is given to theology and race and the black Christian experience in Britain.

The second reason for negative attitudes towards academic theology in the urban context is ignorance and fear. Many Christians still buy into the myth that studying theology will cause a loss of faith or make an individual intellectually confused and spiritually insecure because of the critical and often unnecessary questions they have to engage with. In my experience, fear of academic theology is most evident in churches where the pastor has had little or no formal theological training and feels threatened by members of the congregation advancing theologically. As a result of this fear it is not uncommon in black Pentecostal churches to hear the argument that academic theology is 'mis-education' – placing head knowledge above 'real' Holy Ghost knowledge, the former emerging from books and the latter from experience and knowledge of God. Again, there is some truth in this criticism. Academic theology has often failed to demonstrate that 'having learning does not mean you lose the burning' or enthusiasm for the mission of the Church in the world.

Being a black theologian has at times meant living in double jeopardy; on the one hand, being criticised by academics for bringing 'blackness' to the academic table; on the other hand, being criticised by urban church folk who believe that book learning has limited value for saving souls, building churches and getting a good music ministry going.

Despite this, I have tried to bridge the gap between the urban Church and the academy by 'doing theology' on the intersection between urban church life, black communities and the theological academy. In real terms, my classroom has extended beyond the university and church hall and into prisons, secondary schools and the media. In order to do theology that engages with the urban context it is necessary to construct a relevant theological method.

In this chapter, I want to suggest a particular way of doing theology so that it acts as both a bridge and a weapon. It is a bridge because it brings together the best of the academy and the Church and it is a weapon because it is concerned with addressing in an explicit way the issue of gun crime and gang violence.

The Spiral of Interpretation

My colleagues in pastoral theology introduced me to the spiral of interpretation.[2] Their practical approach gives them a real edge in applying theology and engaging with real-life issues and concerns. The spiral of interpretation is so called because it is a dynamic and transformative process. Liberation theologians have also used pastoral approaches to theology in order to link faith and practice (*praxis*).[3] The spiral has four inter-related parts as illustrated in fig. 1. We will now discuss them more fully in relation to the task of doing theology in the urban context.

Fig. 1

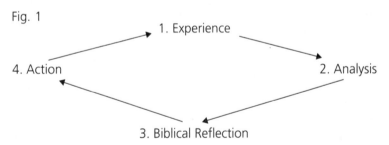

1. Experience

4. Action

2. Analysis

3. Biblical Reflection

Experience

Experience is a crucial starting-point (fig. 1, no. 1). While traditional theology makes the biblical text or a philosophical proposition its existential starting-point, an urban method has to begin with the real-life issues that confront us. If we are committed to justice, peace and liberation in relation to gun crime and gang violence, then we make these issues our starting-point. There are several concerns that must be taken on board.

Firstly, gun culture is part of a wider social failure, as mentioned in the introduction; we can't talk about gangs without reference to structural problems such as educational failure, unemployment or underemployment. Neither can we ignore the underside of global capitalism that has pushed a criminal class out of the Caribbean and Eastern Europe into Britain's metropolitan areas.[4]

Secondly, when examining experience we must consider the ways in which many urban Christian traditions have falsely divided experience into private and public domains, resulting in an inability to recognise and reckon with what is happening outside the Church. The heart of the problem is that within many urban churches worship is viewed as a private and spiritual activity. As a consequence, the public socio-political issues that face us are left at the church doorway. On many occasions I have heard pastors and worship leaders in black urban Pentecostal churches begin a service with the words, 'Let's forget what is happening around us in the world and just concentrate on Jesus.' Sometimes this means that even a mention of social or political issues during the intercessory prayers is shunned. Historically, this separation in African Caribbean experience is the result of a false dichotomy imposed upon blacks during slavery and colonialism.[5]

In contrast, a more effective approach is to see the private and public as one whole rather than as separate entities. When the private and public are unified we can adopt the belief that 'the personal is political'. What I mean here is that what happens to us individually has *wider* social and political ramifications. We need only to consider the personal loss of the family of black teenager Stephen Lawrence to recognise how private grief can have wider political and social implications. The personal struggle of the Lawrence family for justice for their murdered son (a private struggle) was also a quest for communal justice (the reform of the criminal justice system). In response to making the private political in a wider sense, our call to worship should *really* be 'Let's bring all of our concerns to the throne of Grace because we know that our God will speak to us about them today!'

Thirdly, everyone's experiences are not the same. For example the experience of poor whites within the inner city are similar but also dissimilar from their Indian, Bangladeshi, Bengali, Caribbean and West African neighbours. Each community's experience of the police and criminal justice system may bear similarities and differences. A central task must be to find ways of including these varied lived experiences. To this end, dialogue becomes an imperative. This means that while I am dealing with the specifics of black urban cultures in this text, my hope is that those using this book will place it in a critical dialogue with white and Asian theologians exploring the subject from their cultural and social perspectives.

For African Caribbean Christians dialogue across cultural and religious barriers is a particular sticking point. For far too long many black Christians have hidden behind a narrow Christian exclusivity that has limited their ability to be in dialogue with poor whites or Asian members of the community who worship in mosques, temples and gurdwaras. I once went to a meeting held in a black Pentecostal church in Aston, Birmingham, which is a mixed religious and ethnic community. The meeting was an attempt to create a dialogue between the Church and the community. Everyone in the church hall was black African Caribbean and therefore unrepresentative of the wider cultural mix in the locality. Furthermore, everyone who spoke at the meeting was male, again an unrepresentative sample of the African Caribbean community itself. Dialogue across boundaries of class, faith and gender must become an integral dimension of understanding experience if we are to be inclusive. This dialogue will enable us to gain a clearer and broader understanding of the social and political issues that confront us and lead us into the next part of the spiral, social analysis.

Social Analysis

Taking experience seriously requires that we find ways of making sense of what we see, hear and feel. In the past, traditional Western thinking understood the discipline of theology as an objective science which was evaluated using the sources of Scripture and tradition. Human experience was not taken seriously, with the exception of philosophy which was used as a resource for assessing human experience. This meant that the analysis of the human experience and condition was limited by the boundaries and biases of patriarchal Western philosophers. The use of philosophy to mediate theology is still a problem today for many black scholars, especially when you consider that in white male Western philosophy the idea of black people being fully human is a relatively new idea.[6]

In contrast, in liberation theologies such as black theology, concerned with making theology a resource for social change, the social sciences (sociology, politics, economics and cultural studies) come to the fore. This is because amongst liberation theologians it is recognised that theology is contextual or grounded in its social location. This means that theological ideas are shaped by wider cultural, political and social experiences, and because contexts differ, theology will be reshaped accordingly.[7]

The kind of social analysis I am calling for (fig. 1, no. 2) has two central ingredients. Firstly, it means examining a particular social location, looking at individual and group experiences. It also involves examining how individuals and groups live their lives in relationship to wider historical, cultural and political forces. For example, any discussion of black people in Birmingham must examine our history (how and why we are here), our politics (how we relate to each other and social institutions such as government, education and the police) and culture (how we have used our inherited concepts to communicate, challenge and pass on knowledge of life).

Secondly, social analysis is fundamentally about social change. This means that we analyse in order to find out how we can improve the quality of life within a social location. Therefore any social analysis of gun crime must focus on how we can reduce these crimes and find more meaningful ways for young people to engage with the world around them.

Social analysis is not a completely new idea for social workers or social activists. For example, anyone who has worked with offenders, whether in prison chaplaincy or probation work will know that social background has a profound impact on how and why people offend. Neither is this use of analysis, that is, exploring the social context, completely alien to urban churches. Take for example the current explanations for the rise in gun crime in urban areas. Within urban churches I have noted two arguments. There is a conservative 'change your behaviour' camp that believes that the increased use of firearms amongst black youths is due to individual lawlessness and moral and cultural degeneration in the community. For this camp, crime is an individual matter and the solutions are found in stiffer sentences and giving more power to the police. For this group urban blacks in particular are to be policed, controlled and feared. When I hear this argument it saddens me that black church folk are speaking of living in fear of other black people.

An opposing liberal 'must do social work' camp argues that the rise in gun crime is the result of social exclusion. In this camp crime results from a poor social environment and a perceived limited access to society's resources. The solution is found in providing employment and educational opportunities to lift people out of poverty. In this second school, urban black males involved in gun crime are considered passive objects in need of rescue.

However, what is now needed is for both of these schools to appreciate the wider political and historical forces that have shaped the present situation. Both perspectives would benefit from a more complex and sustained analysis, and this is provided in section 2, 'Analysis'. Section 3, 'Biblical Reflection', also identifies the theological benefits to be gained from a broader analytical enterprise.

As mentioned in the introduction, the analytical tools on offer in this book are biased and inevitably reflect my own particular approach towards the gun gang crisis. I believe that while recognising the diversity of urban experience we must begin with an analysis of where we have come from and where we are now. Such a departure means that we need to prioritise exploring the history, politics and economics of colonialism and its effects on contemporary life. As the postcolonial maxim goes: 'We are here because Britain was there!' Postcolonialism is a complex discipline with a specific trajectory for interpreting the cultural, economic and political situation faced by the descendents of colonial subjects in the new inner city 'colonies' of urban Britain.

Colonialism did not only colonise black bodies, but also black minds, so it is imperative to engage in cultural analysis. Aspects of cultural analysis enable us to explore the complex ways in which black cultures have been mobilised in response to the mental colonisation and the neo-colonialism (new forms of colonial activity) that confront us. As mentioned in the introduction, culture is the new front line, as the struggle over black representation is the strategic battlefield where the re-articulation of white superiority and the perception of the black community are being fought.

We can't let white people off the hook in our social analysis. This is why I have included a brief study of 'whiteness'. I am particularly concerned with how whiteness has been intimately linked to power within British history. Unlocking the workings of whiteness enables us to make sense of how racialised oppression occurs in new subtle and unseen forms. However, social analysis must also address identity politics within black communities, that is, the historical values and traditions that enable oppressed communities to survive and thrive despite the odds stacked against them. Afrocentricity provides a useful insight in this regard by offering a framework for communal identity politics within which economic, political and cultural struggle can be initiated.

Once we have engaged in social analysis, our next task is to take what we have learned to the Scriptures.

Biblical Reflection

The next stage of the spiral is biblical reflection (fig. 1, no. 3). Whereas social analysis addresses aspects of our condition, biblical reflection considers what the Word of God has to say about our situation. Using the results of our social analysis, we are able to go deeper in our engagement with the text and hope to find substantial answers to the questions raised by our analysis. It is partly because of superficial theological reflection that many churches in the urban context have tended to provide superficial answers to the questions that confront us. Without serious social analysis we fail to bring to the Word of God the depth and breadth of the concerns that face us in the world today.

Armed with new cultural or political insights from social analysis, there are several tasks that we need to undertake. Firstly, we need to reinterpret the Bible. Such a reinterpretation must be the outcome of an engagement or meeting of the horizons of our experience with the Scriptures. This may seem harsh or bold to those used to reading the Bible as a perfect guidebook. However, according to every major study, urban churches using the 'perfect guidebook' method over the last twenty years have failed to engage critically with the social and political issues facing urban people.[8] It is time to undertake a new way of reading Scripture which fully recognises social analysis.

To assist with reinterpretation, I advocate reader response and ideological interpretive tools as the preferred method of unlocking issues of power and justice in the Bible. Reader response places the socio-political life experiences of the reader in a critical conversation with the socio-political realities behind the Scriptures. Ideological interpretation takes to task the issues of power and powerlessness in Scripture and considers the implications for power dynamics in the urban situation. For example, reading the story of the Exodus from a reader response perspective enables urban people to place their socio-political concerns in dialogue with a God of socio-political liberation. In the Exodus, God is presented as a God of social and political liberation who frees an oppressed people (the Hebrews) from economic and political bondage in Egypt. Rereading the same passage from an ideological perspective raises a new set of questions. Consider for a moment that when God liberated the Hebrew people they still carried their slaves with them into the wilderness (Exodus 20:22–23:33). One interpretation of this passage is as a warning to us in the present; oppressed people should consider if their quest for freedom should ever be fulfilled at the expense of others.

The result of this religious reflection should be to encourage us to look afresh at our experiences and propel us into new forms of action.

Action

When talking about action, I am thinking of various activities. Action refers to:

- educating, informing and teaching.
- proclaiming or making public the convictions that arise through analysis and biblical reflection.
- advocacy: engaging with the political system in order to work for change. This may involve writing to politicians or supporting local initiatives such as those aimed at preventing gun crime.
- organising: working with existing bodies and establishing new groups that will co-operate and work together to change the social environment. Organising may involve marches and other days of action aimed at empowering the community to challenge gunmen and gang members.

The action outlined above is not the final part of this spiral but is relevant at every stage of the spiral (fig 1, no. 4). For example, exploring experience or doing analysis may prompt us to act upon what we have learned even before we approach Scripture. On many occasions I have found myself acting upon a particular experience before serious analysis has occurred. Even so, I make sure I return to the spiral to benefit from it. In essence, the kind of action we are engaging with here is a form of action–reflection, where thought is not separate from action but an integral part of it. This is what is meant by the term *praxis*. Put simply, action in this system is a targeted response to the outcome of social analysis and biblical reflection and therefore occurs throughout the process.

Action to change the social environment for the better takes place on a number of levels; the street or community level, the level of the church and the municipal level. The street level is concerned with making the streets safer by reducing crime and improving the quality of the physical environment. Probably the best existing example of this level of action is present in the work of the Street Pastor mission in London and the Young Disciples in Birmingham. (These are discussed in more detail in chapter 11.)

The church level is concerned with preaching, teaching and tailoring ministries to respond actively to the new under-standing. Finally at the municipal level action for change is concerned with the mechanics of lobbying and challenging local government to 'do the right thing'. The goal of action at the municipal level is to ensure social change at a political level. In Birmingham and other cities there are already local councillors working at the forefront of the struggle for more racially just cities. However, the spiral does not end with action, because action generates new experiences that must be analysed and reflected upon – thus beginning the process anew.

In summary, in order to address meaningfully gun crime and gang violence it is necessary to develop a theological method which is able to fully embrace the range of challenges presented. I have advocated the use of the hermeneutical spiral as a way of taking the crisis (experience) to the biblical text (biblical reflection) informed by religious–cultural analysis of the situation (social analysis). The aim is to produce ongoing action informed by experience, analysis and reflection.

Study Questions
- Do you think there is a fear of academic theology in many black urban churches in Britain? Why?
- What is the role of your personal experiences in shaping your ideas about God? Are there limits to the use of experience as a measure of what God is doing in the world?

- What is the role of analysis? How can it help to make sense of our experiences?
- What are the tasks involved in biblical reflection?
- What is action–reflection? What are the different levels on which action can occur?

Chapter 2

Are You Listening?

Experience As Our Starting-Point

In the previous chapter, we outlined a theological method that we can use to investigate systemic failure. In this chapter, we will explore in greater detail the importance of beginning our theological investigation with experience.

To talk about personal experience is to talk about the events, feelings and concerns we encounter that shape our perception and awareness. Experience can be personal as well as communal; my own experience of being African Caribbean is both personal and communal. I have individual experiences that are particular to myself, but I also share experiences common to many African Caribbean men of my generation. Experience varies from individual to individual. My experience of schooling in Britain will not be the same as every other African Caribbean person of my age and class; experience is often contradictory, and it can be mixed. So at an individual level, differences in background, class, relationships and education all work to create different social, psychological and cognitive experiences.

Because the experiences we have influence how we live, think and act, the influence of experience (personal and communal) on how we do theology in the world today should also be acknowledged. The construction of theological ideas cannot be separated from human experience. I would contend that the incarnation (John 1:14) affirms the importance of human experience in salvation history (God's intervention to save humanity), as it was necessary for God to engage with human experience in and through the humanity of Jesus in order to communicate what it means to be a follower of God. The story of Jesus and his encounters with the rich and poor show us how God uses human experience to communicate divine revelation. So even in Scripture, human experience is a factor in how God reveals what is right and wrong in the world and what humans must do to improve their personal and social environments.

However, traditionalists in theology have avoided grappling with the contentious issue of personal experience when 'doing theology'. There are at least two reasons for this.

Firstly, European theology, the dominant academic theological tradition, has advocated an objective approach to theological reflection. Objective scholarship, the task of good theologians in the West, is partly concerned with not allowing your biased experiences to get in the way of what you are examining. Consequently, when theologising, scholars must set aside personal experience in a quest for objectivity. For this reason, theologians in European history have described their work as 'Christian Theology' rather than contextualising it according to the experiences that have shaped it, such as white, male and middle class experience.

Secondly, theologians have not acknowledged the role of experience because of the political implications of doing so. If experience is understood to influence theological discussions and pronouncements, then it is logical to conclude that every theologian's biases will affect their understanding. Accepting prior bias in theological reflection would mean that theologians would no longer be able to portray theology as an objective pursuit. Scholarly awareness of this reality has led to new ways of doing theology that acknowledge, celebrate and seek to make central particular individual and group experiences. Hence the advent of black, gay, evangelical, conservative, feminist and other 'biased' theologies.[1]

There are advantages to be gained by making experience a lens through which theology is explored. It is a more democratic way of theologising, as everyone's experience is considered to be valid and worthy of dialogue with Scripture. We are also more likely to get to the heart of pressing issues by allowing personal and communal experience to impact theology in an implicit way. For example, the discipline of black theology makes black experience its starting-point in order to address the concerns of black people. Likewise, womanist theology addresses the experiences of black women. Finally, personal experience enables us to find new meanings within the Bible. As we shall see later, 'reader response' interpretation is based upon taking seriously the concerns and experience of each reader of the Bible in order to draw out new meanings.

The major disadvantage of prioritising experience at the beginning of the theological task is that without the mediating benefit of tradition and reason it can lead to dangerous, destructive and errant theological interpretations. What I am identifying here is the relationship between the *particular* and the *universal*. While we may begin with experiences that are specific to a given context, we are obliged theologically to recognise universal significance. In this case, beginning with the particularity of the systemic failure that leads to an outlaw culture amongst sections of the urban community must lead to a universal truth and practice about the nature and being of God. But history serves a warning about unmediated experience – church people who supported Apartheid in South Africa were driven and informed by their particular experiences of the past (Boer history) but neglected the reason and tradition and produced a corrupt reading of Scripture that supported white supremacy. Therefore, experience must never be accepted unchallenged or without an engagement with universal notions of human integrity and value.

Experience and Knowing in Black Faith (Epistemology)

Experience is an important value in black faith. In my church upbringing in Britain, a deep personal and living 'experience of God' was considered central to one's faith. This fact became clear when I returned home after my undergraduate theological studies. The letters after my name did not impress members of the church, who had raised me in my faith. They were more interested in the measure of faith I had developed as a result of my experience of God as a student. Valuing religious experience in this way tells us something profound about the 'ways of knowing' (epistemology) in the black Pentecostal church tradition in which I was raised; experience of God is at the centre of religious meaning. To have knowledge of God (theology) is secondary to knowing God (a living experience). This is one of the primary foci of worship in black Pentecostal churches. Through ecstatic, expressive, spiritual worship, prayer, praise and preaching, members are encouraged to 'experience God'. In fact, the presence of God is measured by the intensity of the worship.

What I want to suggest in this chapter is that urban churches must also give a similar priority to experience outside the Church in order to interpret more effectively the ways that God is at work in individuals and groups in the social world.

Racism, Experience and the Urban Church

It is important to remember that people in the Church live social lives. They live in a secular society, work in varied and diverse professions and are often part of an oppressed ethnic group. It is therefore fundamental that urban churches do not neglect what happens outside specific church experience (worship, prayer meetings and fellowship) and instead examine all experience in response to the liberating message of the Gospel. The classic example of neglecting to do this is the failure of black urban pastors to preach about racism in an explicit and informed way. In over thirty years of listening to sermons in urban churches, I have yet to hear a meaningful or convincing sermon on what the Bible has to say about racism.

Sadly, a central feature of black life in Britain has been ubiquitous racialised oppression. Black men and women use a variety of ways of outmanoeuvring various forms of racism, both personal and communal. Some avoid the subject, others engage with it head-on. But most negotiate daily assaults, choosing where and when to fight their battles. Some of these strategies are historic, based on traditions forged during the resistance to slavery and colonialism;[2] other strategies have been 'made in

Britain' during the past fifty years of black presence.[3] The issue that concerns us here is the way in which black urban churches have responded to the experience of racism. There have been at least two approaches. The first is *internalised resistance* and the second, *transcendence*.

Internalised resistance refers to empowerment of the individual and group as a means of contesting and destroying racial myths and practice. The idea here is that through moral and educational improvement, the controlling effects of racist stereotypes are neutralised.[4] In practice this has meant that the local church encourages its members to be upright, good citizens, hard workers and educational achievers. Consequently, black urban churches, particularly African churches, have a high percentage of graduates, professionals and independent business people.

Transcendence refers to the capacity of urban Church theology for living above and beyond 'race'. In black urban churches there exists a tradition of dissolving 'racial' differences into a spiritual brother- and sisterhood of faith. When you become a Christian your Christian identity takes priority over ethnicity and culture.[5] One of the reasons why many black Christians and church leaders dispute the description 'black church' is because they have transcended ethnic categories in their individual and group self-recognition. But in practice this approach is simply a form of avoidance that does not actively confront racism inside or outside the Church. Only through an active engagement that unites personal improvement with campaigning and action can racism and other forms of discrimination be checked.

In contrast, I would like to propose a 'politicised' understanding of our experience. This means that as well as empowering individuals (internal resistance) and living above racialised oppression (transcendence) we must also be explicitly active in analysing and addressing the causes of oppression. This is needed for 'experience' to work effectively as a starting-point for doing theology in response to systemic failure. We can't ignore what we see or dismiss what we hear!

The politicisation of experience is a way of talking about experience in relationship to issues of power and exclusion. This is not a new idea in Christian thought. The Bible itself is full of examples of the politicisation of experience. Returning to the example of the incarnation, we may say that the Son of God being sent to earth as a colonised person (a first-century Jew) who undergoes the death of a political agitator (the cross) is a political act on the part of God. In a similar vein, today womanist (black feminist) theology politicises the experience of black women. Race, class and gender oppression are brought to the centre of their theological discussion in order to explore how theology can be a tool for liberation for black women in oppressive situations in North America, Europe, the Caribbean and Africa.[6]

There are three ways in which urban churches can engage with experience and thereby become better equipped to make experience the starting-point for doing theology.

Past Experience

The first way is through engagement with the past. More specifi-cally, I am concerned with the historic role the Church has played in resistance against oppression. In colonial histories, the church of the colonised was often a strategic player in the fight against colonisation. In the Caribbean for example, the nineteenth century is full of a multitude of Christian men and women such as Sam Sharpe and Amy Garvey (Jamaica) who believed that God's commitment to the downtrodden was a mandate to work for social change, that is, the end of colonialism. The high point of this tradition is found in the twentieth century with the central role the churches played in the fight against Apartheid in South Africa and segregation in the Civil Rights struggle in America.

The concept of political urban churches full of 'people of colour' united and working for a better community is part of the history of many urban churches today. For example, the Baptist Church in Jamaica was one of the most radical opponents of slavery and colonisation in the Christian tradition.[7] By excavating these hidden histories, urban churches can find models and ideas of what it means to politicise experience in order to engage more effectively with and change the social world in which we live.

Present Experience

The second way concerns the type of dialogue we have with present experience. While there exists a vast array of contexts with which we might engage, I want to prioritise the (black) Atlantic network. Whether we like it or not, American church culture and theology has had a profound effect on urban church life in Britain. The advent of satellite television beaming in American preachers and church services has only served to increase the reliance on North America as a source of theological inspiration. Dialogue and exchange between black people in Africa, the Americas and Europe has a long history. The 'golden triangle' of the transatlantic slave trade which shipped slaves and goods from Africa to the New World was also a communication network. This network has survived into the present in the form of an 'Atlantic culture' and specifically a black Atlantic exchange network.[8] What I want to advocate is a theological conversation that goes beyond swapping preachers, evangelistic crusades and church planting techniques. We need a serious and protracted dialogue on how the urban Church can live out its mandate successfully in localities blighted by poverty, unemployment and gun crime. Urban churches in London, Birmingham and Manchester need to build relationships with inner city churches in the USA which have a successful record of addressing and resisting oppressive forces both inside and outside the community. Unfortunately, at present it is still the superstar evangelists of megachurch fame who get the top billing amongst many urban churches in the UK. While these individuals may have much to offer, generally they lack the experience and understanding of how Atlantic cultures sustain, support and nurture each other in the face of systemic failure.

Future Experience

One of the main sources of inspiration for urban churches is the future hope that Jesus is coming and that his return will put things right. A multitude of songs, testimonies and prayers sung, exhorted and spoken at services focus on the future as the end of time. So the final area of exchange concerns the politicisation of the future – as Pentecostals might say, we need to have a 'vision'. For the Caribbean diaspora, eschatological (future) hope enabled our slave ancestors see beyond the immediate problems or obstacles and believe that 'betta mus cum' (better must come). Christian churches are called to be future-oriented. This means hoping for and believing that better prospects will come along eventually. Because we know how the 'story ends', we live our lives inspired and assured.

The dialogue with the future and its reality in Scripture enables us to dream, hope and rest assured that in the words of many a gospel song 'a better day is coming'. By politicising future experience, dreaming and hoping that better will come, our task in the present takes on new meaning and purpose. In short, we are part of God's political redemptive plan for our communities. Therefore we have to be able to identify what the future will look like and what we need to do to achieve communities free of systemic failure, gun crime and gang violence.

However, dialogue with the future has often led to complacency in the present. Many urban churches have dreamed of the world to come (heaven) at the expense of their prophetic mandate in this world (building the Kingdom of God). This is the 'pie in the sky' mentality. In response, the kind of dialogue with the future that I am nurturing is one that inspires us to act and do the necessary work for change. In other words, we work to make the future kingdom that is becoming a reality here and now. It was this hope (a realised eschatology) that drove Martin Luther King to work in the present, aware of the dream for the future. Naturally, we know that not everything can be accomplished here and now; we may not end gun crime tomorrow. But our dialogue with the future also informs us that this world is not all that there is and that better will come.

Experience and Gun Crime

The focus of this book is gun crime and gang violence. So when making experience a theological starting-point we have to bring to the fore the complex experiential issues at work.

One aspect is psychological. I refer here to the personal experiences that result in nihilistic actions – what Cornel West calls meaninglessness and hopelessness that produce lovelessness.[9] For example, when I work in prison with young working-class men, they often refer to their criminal motivation being related to a lack of positive examples in their environment to challenge the general lack of direction, self-esteem or hope.

Another major factor is structural. This is the social context that produces nihilism. It is a well-known sociological fact that poverty and educational underachievement (structural forces) influence the potential for criminality, including gun crime.[10] Many young people feel trapped by a poor education and limited job prospects.

Finally, another feature of systemic failure that must be central to our theological task is culture. It is vital to consider the cultural values at work in a social situation. These include the special status given to the criminal, justification for the acquisition of material goods such as elaborate jewellery, prestigious brand cars and designer clothing, and the kudos associated with bearing arms. All these are important social and cultural factors.[11]

Psychological, structural and cultural features must feature in any meaningful evaluation of this particular 'experience'. Psychological matters enable us to address the internal forces behind gun crime and gang violence, structural matters enable us to address the systemic failure that impacts upon it, and cultural factors enable us to get to grips with the meaning and values at work. These three features are not independent of each other but inter-related.

In summary, in this chapter I have argued that experience is an important theological category. That is to say, it must be the starting-point for investigating the meaning of God in the world. Experience must be politicised; we need to make the experience of injustice and deprivation concrete issues that are central to the task of doing theology. The psychological and structural matters at the heart of systemic failure should weigh heavily on our theological minds.

Study Questions

- How have your personal experiences such as family life, schooling and ethnic background shaped your theology?
- How have the experiences of migration, racism, employment or criminality impacted on your church?
- Do you believe that politicising experience is a positive pursuit for Christians?
- Which do you feel has the greatest impact on gun crime and gang violence; behavioural, structural or cultural experiences?

SECTION 2

Analysis

Chapter 3

Old and New Colonies

The Continued Impact of Colonialism

The aim of this section is to offer an overview of the broad frameworks that go some way towards explaining the economic, cultural and political factors at play in the gun crime and gang violence phenomenon. As mentioned in chapter 2, experience must be evaluated and the analytical tools we use influence and shape how we understand our experiences. This chapter begins with an exploration of postcolonial analysis, while the following chapters in this section explore cultural and Afrocentric analysis and critical white studies.

I want to begin with a story. I participated in two community events covered by the media in the aftermath of the new year shootings of the two cousins in Birmingham. The first was a televised event for the local Carlton *Evening News*. Despite the actual event being a varied mix of comment and exhortation, it was interesting that the report which was broadcast covered selected vehement statements made at the meeting and in particular highlighted angry exchanges between several of the African Caribbean people present. The second event was a live radio broadcast on BBC Radio 5. During the broadcast there was a sense of unease amongst the black audience as they felt that the presenter Nicky Campbell had misunderstood their perspectives. Consequently some chose to leave the building. Unaware of what was happening, and misinterpreting the situation, the programme's presenter claimed that a 'scuffle was breaking out' amongst the predominantly black audience. This mistake went uncorrected on air and left a distorted impression of the character of those at the meeting.

Both media broadcasts conveyed a sense that when black people are gathered together to discuss issues it happens in an environment that is violent, angry and irrational. Such images of black people are not recent media creations, but have a long history in the British context. In this chapter, I want to argue that it is necessary to analyse the systemic failure responsible for gun crime and gang violence within a wider historical context, namely colonialism.

As we shall see, analysing the continued impact of colonialism (postcolonialism) enables us to look afresh at how the past affects the present. In this case it enables us to rethink how black people, including Christians, have been represented and have internalised representations that are rooted in a racist and brutal past. We begin by defining what is meant by postcolonialism and its characteristics, after which we will explore how colonialism continues to have an impact upon the urban context in structuring the ways in which black and other minorities are treated and represented in Britain.

Postcolonialism

What does it mean to talk about postcolonialism? Postcolonialism is a critical reflection on how colonialism worked in the past and its continued impact on us today. It has a variety of features.

Firstly, it concerns the ways in which colonial powers developed policies, practices and images to maintain their positions of power. While we recognise that British imperialism took on a variety of forms in various locations, for African and African Caribbean folk, colonialism was negatively defined by a history of slavery and racial terror. Any sensible black person will confess that these features have not completely disappeared but have been reworked and disguised in contemporary discourse on former colonial subjects such as African Caribbean people in Britain. Anwar Sivanandan, an eminent social analyst, once described the situation faced by African and Asian people in Britain as a 'domestic neocolonial situation'.[1] Put simply, Sivanandan argues that we live in a new colonial context, where the practices and policies of nineteenth- and early twentieth-century colonialism are simply reconfigured and updated to meet the needs of today.

But poor whites also suffered under colonialism. This is why in recent revisions of the British Empire, scholars have also stressed the impact of Caribbean colonisation on poor whites who were pressganged, indentured and sometimes brutalised to further the dominant class position of the slave-owning plantation élite. Even so, the most enduring feature of colonial power and practice is how race continues to be a salient feature of urban life in Britain today.

Secondly, to talk of postcolonialism is to explore black resistance. This would entail an examination of how former colonial subjects engaged with and also transformed colonial practices, policies and images in order to oppose, resist and liberate themselves from the implicit and explicit hold of colonisation.[2] This second category refers to anticolonial struggles in the past (Indian and African liberation struggles) and present (antiracism).

Considering the past, in Caribbean history we might consider the work and lives of figures such as Marcus and Amy Garvey, Claudia Jones, Frantz Fanon and C. L. R. James. In contemporary Britain we can also view the work of the family of Stephen Lawrence as part of a continued struggle against new forms of colonialism.

The third task of postcolonial criticism is to place colonialism at the centre of our discussions on race and ethnicity – in other words, to interpret what happened to us on the plantations and what takes place on the streets, in the workplaces and the schools in Britain as a continuum. Postcolonial, political, cultural, economic and social analysis of systemic failure is therefore grounded in the profound sense of a continuing process of discrimination, oppression and hostility by the descendents of former colonial powers towards the descendents of their former colonial subjects. The recent 'trendy' reappraisals of colonialism in books and television programmes by revisionist historians such as Niall Ferguson[3] all too clearly remind black people that the full brutality and enduring influence of colonialism is still *not* completely understood or appreciated in contemporary Britain.

Domestic Neocolonialism

It is important to remember that British colonialism differed within each social context and evolved over time. For example, the Irish experience was different from the experience of first nation people in Australia and Canada. Even so, there are shared experiences and these are the issues and values that Sivanandan would want us to explore.

I believe that existing areas of contemporary black urban lives have real resonance with the colonial past. I want to look at four colonial resonances and how they continue to impact on African and African Caribbean people; economics, mentality, culture and religion.

Economics

Colonisation was fundamentally a form of economic exploitation. Black and brown peoples were put to work by force to feed the economic needs of British and other European colonialists. A trail of exploitation in the experience of African Caribbean people such as myself begins with slavery in the Caribbean, extends into the colonial era of the nineteenth century and finds contemporary expression in the post World War II period as Caribbean migrants travelled to Britain in search of work. As Winston James and Clive Harris have demonstrated, colonialism produced a cheap and plentiful labour supply in the Caribbean.[4] Moreover, many second- and third-generation black British people such as myself identify today's disproportionate unemployment rates and the high incidence of underemployment amongst African Caribbean men and women in Britain as the present manifestation of a long, almost seamless history of economic exploitation.[5]

Psychological Slavery

The greatest assault on Africans was at the psychological level, with attempts not only to make blacks feel inferior, but to have them internalise their inferiority and act it out on each other. This was the real skill of Caribbean colonisation according to the scholarly work of Martinique's Frantz Fanon. Fanon has had a profound impact on increasing awareness of the devastating psychological legacy of colonisation amongst former colonial subjects. In particular, Fanon identifies how colonialism bred a sense of inadequacy and dependence that was still present amongst the descendents of colonial subjects.[6] More recently, African-centred scholars have added to the analysis of internalised racism but focused on the features, structures and content of European thought and practice geared up to control and manufacture a sense of inferiority amongst black and other oppressed ethnic groups. To this end the reflections of black feminist scholar, Patricia Hill Collins are an invaluable contribution to this area of study.[7] Hill identifies intellectual traditions constructed amongst white men in Europe and America (the Eurocentric masculinist validation process), structured to dismiss and ignore the intellectual capacity and traditions of African Americans and other diasporan blacks. On a popular level, the Rastafarian Movement in the Caribbean and Britain and politically-conscious hip-hop artists in America and Europe have also explored in song and visual art the 'mental slavery' that accompanied the physical form. The canons of Bob Marley (reggae), Michael Franti and Spearhead (hip-hop) are good examples from each genre.

The internalisation of oppression was, on one level, a form of psychological brain-washing geared towards enslaving the mind as well as the body, what Bob Marley termed 'mental slavery'. It was a systematic dehumanisation based on aesthetics (you are ugly), cognition (you are stupid), and esteem (you are worthless). People who believed themselves to be animalistic, stupid and self-destructive would act out behaviour that would be of little threat to the prevailing order. Later in colonial history blacks progressed from being portrayed and treated as if they were part human to being viewed as childlike. For this reason, a black man or woman in colonial society continued to be called a 'boy' or a 'girl' no matter how old they were.

Mental slavery, or internalised racism, is still a hot topic amongst African Caribbean men and women in the neocolonial context of contemporary Britain. Faced with a continued negative discourse on black inferiority structured around notions of blacks being more physical (for example, sports), dangerous (criminal) and only viable as entertainers (comedians), many believe that colonial images and values are encoded in discussions on race, identity, immigration and asylum.[8]

Tragically, in the postcolonial context, there are still benefits to be gained by 'blacking up' or playing up to the negative preconceived role expected of black people. For example, the plethora of black entertainers in the public spotlight (television presenters, singers and other entertainers) inadvertently suggest to the black community that 'blacking up' is a legitimate way to be successful. One may argue that there is a similar process at work amongst many youths involved in gun crime and gang violence. In short, they are simply internalising and reproducing stereotypes of what young black disaffected men are expected to do within a postcolonial situation. According to postcolonial psychology, the internalisation of negative racist representations of the black self manifests itself in a form of 'self-hate'. Self-hate was after all, an express aim of colonialism – to get the colonial subject to believe in his or her own inferiority and also to act it out as a reality.[9]

Culture

The attempts by European colonisers to destroy African identity also included an attack on its cultures. Put simply, intellectual resources, books, art and sciences were put to work to prove that African cultures were inferior and therefore barbaric.[10] In the hierarchy of cultural progress, Africans were placed at the bottom of the achievement pyramid. If Africans were to be given any attributes of enduring value then they were generally physical and sexual. We were perceived as strong workers and good childbearers who enjoyed dancing and beating drums. Physicality was a compensation for what Africans were believed to lack intellectually.[11]

Myths of African sexual potency were often the basis for brutal and savage repression of black males in the colony. Some scholars have gone as far to suggest that this cultural assault was not all that new, but went back to negative assessments of Africans that began as early as Greco-Roman times.[12] Later on in colonial history, pseudo-science was introduced in order to legitimise the belief in African intellectual inferiority. Measures of physiques, head sizes and facial shapes were introduced to evaluate cultural superiority and inferiority. Naturally these measures were biased to ensure that the British and Europeans came out on top and the Africans at the bottom,[13] enabling science to validate a social Darwinism (superior humans will dominate inferior ones).

In contemporary Britain black expressive cultures are still a site of contested importance. From a postcolonial perspective influenced by power dynamics and the impact of the past, it could be argued that it is often the physical forms (dance, music) of self-expression that have dominated as opposed to the literary forms (writing, scholarship), leaving most people knowing more about black singers and comedians than black writers, scientists and intellectuals. This is not to say that these expressive cultures cannot be politicised to challenge the status quo. We know this because there is a long history in Black Atlantic cultures of men and women interpreting cultural expression so as to challenge perceptions of ability and attainment.[14] This contest is also witnessed within the broader context where black expressive cultures hold a contradictory place in popular culture. On the one hand they are actively pursued and copied as an authentic expression of 'cool'. But they are also demonised and blamed for nihilistic behaviour in urban communities. The colonial legacy of exoticising and demonising the black 'other' is therefore still played out on many cultural fronts.

Religion

Finally, central to the colonial task was divine justification of the white supremacist social order. To keep African people from challenging the power structure it was necessary to provide an ideology of oppression. What I mean by this is a system of ideas that justify black subordination and its enforcement. Although there was some resistance amongst small groups of missionaries, Christian religion eventually occupied this role. With the advent of European missionaries to the Caribbean and Africa, unscrupulous theologians in Europe pronounced that God was *for* slavery. They based their arguments on bogus readings of the Curse of Ham (Genesis 9), and a belief that black skin signified divine disfavour and possibly the 'mark of Cain' (Genesis 4). Missionaries were therefore able to pronounce divine support for the enslavement of millions of Africans. For the slaves, the best they could hope for was that by 'obeying their masters' (Colossians 3:22) they would receive a great reward in heaven. Even today, urban churches have not untangled themselves from this colonial legacy.

The impact of colonialism on religion continues into the present in Britain. Scholars have argued that while African and African Caribbean churches in Britain may be black on the outside, they still have a white centre dominated by colonial ideas and images.[15] There are several theories as to how and why this continues to be the case. In *Dread and Pentecostal*, I explore some of these reasons through an analysis of black urban churches' perspectives on political action.[16]

The prophetic role of the Church is another area where the colonial past impacts upon us. Black Christianity in Britain, while offering a platform for social advancement and educational achievement amongst African and African Caribbean folk, has failed to pursue actively a political or prophetic role which challenges the social structures responsible for limiting black life. Many would argue that the inability to develop a holistic approach to God's liberating work (concern with souls and the social world) is a direct result of false dichotomies of the private and public role of religion imposed by missionary theology (see chapter 1). As a consequence, the jury is still out on the ability of the urban Church to have a meaningful impact on the quest for justice in urban Britain.

Resisting Colonialism, Resisting Gun Crime

As mentioned above, mapping the form and content of colonial resistance is one dimension of postcolonialism. Postcolonial scholars point out that despite subjugation and oppression colonial subjects and their neocolonial counterparts such as black Britons have always found ways of resisting mental, cultural and religious oppression. Regarding the subjugation of black people, every good student of African and Caribbean history will know that African slaves did not comply with negative representations of Africans in the European intellectual and popular traditions without resistance. African men and women found ways to retain a sense of selfhood and pride despite the oppressive onslaught on their identity. Similarly, the attack on African culture was severely resisted. Blacks found ways of retaining their cultural heritage away from the gaze of the plantocracy (the ruling élite during slavery) and succeeding colonial rulers. The 'African soul' lived on despite persistent attempts to destroy African identities and cultures.[17]

Religion was also a tool for resistance on a variety of levels from rebellion to nonviolent subversion. In Caribbean history the nineteenth century is full of brave acts by Christian-inspired slave men and women who interpreted their faith as a divine justification for the freedom of all people.[18] However, these traditions of Christian-inspired quests for social justice are less evident and commonplace in traditional Caribbean Christianity in the twentieth century. Some scholars argue that it was in the marginal movements such as Rastafarianism that black Caribbean liberation theology was nurtured in the last century.[19]

While the legacy of black Christian political radicalism is not celebrated in urban churches, it has not been forgotten in black theological circles. Black political theologies of the Caribbean, Americas and Europe is built on the heritage of the resistance and rebellion of black Christian slaves.[20]

In relation to the systemic failure reflected in gun crime and gang violence, postcolonialism offers a specific analysis.

Fundamentally, systemic failure must be placed within the rubric of economic exploitation. A lack of social amenities and educational resources, together with racist policing and the assault on culture are the new ways of keeping black folks in check. Similarly, the popular media image of black people as limited to only violent or comedic activity is interpreted from a postcolonial gaze as an inherent dimension of entrenched racism in the white ruling British psyche. Consequently, representing black people as either criminals or entertainers is, from a postcolonial perspective, a systematic attempt to limit and control black life. Those involved in gun crime and gang violence are on one level internalising and living out postcolonial oppression. From this perspective a black youth holding and using a gun is not an expression of power or an outlaw mentality but an example of the postcolonial system winning the battle to control black people.

Postcolonial analysis seeks to redeem the situation through developing and articulating resistance strategies; in short, mobilising mental, cultural and religious resources to refute and dismantle colonialism's continued influence.

In response to postcolonial analysis the task of the urban Church is to be postcolonial. Every urban church should take a 'colonisation audit' that explores how the values and images of the colonial past impact on their worship and practice. The easiest way to get to grips with this matter is to ask the question, 'How is race addressed in this congregation?' A colonial church never addresses racism and sees itself as colour blind despite the facts of the last four hundred years. A more sophisticated audit can occur through reading black theological explorations of the impact of colonialism on the black church in the Caribbean and Britain.

In *Jesus is Dread,* I suggest that the greatest colonial legacy is found in the inability of urban churches to politicise their faith; that is, to develop explicit forms of political engagement on behalf of black communities under siege. The reason for this is the reluctance to let go of the slave master's religious proclamation that we should not worry about our life on earth because 'everything will be all right in heaven'.[21]

In summary, in this chapter I have set out a postcolonial analysis as a tool for analysing the experience of systemic failure. Postcolonialism informs us that systemic failure is not new; it is part of a wider discourse designed to keep former colonial subjects 'in their place'. Furthermore, from the vantage point of postcolonial analysis many of those engaged in gun crime and gang violence have internalised a negative racialised self-image and are playing it out to devastating effect. Postcolonial analysis demands that the urban Church examines itself in order to develop a postcolonial perspective capable of decolonising its theology.

Study Questions
- What is your understanding of colonialism?
- To what extent do you agree with the thesis that colonialism continues to have an impact on urban culture, politics and psyches in Britain today?
- What would you consider to be the characteristics of a colonised mind?
- How does colonialism continue to influence urban churches today?
- Draw up a list of points which you feel should be included in an urban church's colonisation audit.
- Identify traditions of resistance amongst African Caribbean people and explore ways in which they could become part of a decolonised theology.

Chapter 4

More than Just a Bass Line

Cultural Analysis

Kim Howells (then Culture minister), commenting on the rise of gun crime in black communities in the aftermath of the shootings in January 2003 claimed that rap music was partly responsible,[1] suggesting that the young men responsible for the killings were under the influence of rap music produced by bands such as UK rap collective So Solid Crew. This is not a new idea amongst politicians, the police and social commentators in Britain. I can remember that during the 1980s in Britain another black music genre, Ragamuffin, was blamed for a rise in so-called 'Yardie' (Jamaican) crime in Britain. The basic presupposition that underpins the perceived causal relationship between crime and black urban music is that violent images and lyrics in songs and music videos have a negative psychological effect on those listening and watching, especially the young. The young and impressionable are thought to be ill-equipped to distinguish between fact and fiction in rap lyrics and video images. Black social commentators suggest that young, urban and poor black youths, with limited access to educational resources and positive role models are especially vulnerable.[2]

Kim Howells' comments went generally unanswered by black church leaders despite the statement being a classic misunderstanding of the complex meanings within black expressive cultures. As we shall see below, to talk of black expressive cultures as good or bad is not always helpful as it fails to capture their complexities, contradictions and meanings. Not all black culture is bad and certainly not all rap music is negative.

We will begin with a brief examination of the concept of culture, and then explore how churches and Christian workers can constructively engage with urban cultures.

Culture

The word culture was originally a way of describing the farming of land, that is, *cultivation*. But in recent years it has taken on additional meanings. It is for instance the product of a pro- gramme of improved behaviour and learned appreciation of the 'finer things in life'. This is why we say that a person is 'cultured'. Some people view culture as inherited values, attitudes and ways of understanding. According to this perspective, culture is therefore the possession of a particular ethnic group or class of people. Hence the term *black culture*, indicating that it is the property of a particular group. But the most useful way of thinking about culture is as a system of communication (signification) that informs and challenges the social order.[3] This means that culture:

- is something that we create: it is part of our everyday lives.
- has values and moralities expressed in and through it.
- can be used to repress, to uplift or to challenge the way things are.

Obviously it is not possible to discuss every feature of black urban culture here but there are some useful guides for this study.

Scholars such as Michael Eric Dyson, Paul Gilroy and bell hooks identify the diverse range of culture forms that exist within black communities in the USA and Britain. You only have to travel to Dalston Market in London on a Saturday to see diverse groups of black people from the Caribbean, Africa, Latin America, North America and Britain. Therefore we should really talk about black 'cultures' in the plural rather than one black culture. However, despite the diversity there are some simi- larities. If you go into an average black music shop you will see music from all over the world in many different styles and forms, but they are all considered 'black' because they have roots in, and are related to, the history and culture of Africans on the continent and abroad (diaspora). To identify the connectedness of black music forms, ethnomusicologists have uncovered the ways in which beats, rhythms and styles found in rap, reggae and jazz amongst diaspora African communities in America and Europe originated with African slaves transported to the New World during the transatlantic slave trade.[4]

A second feature that is as important to note is that black cultures are not the sole property of black people. This is because black cultural forms are borrowed and reproduced by people who are not black. For instance in May 2003, the England soccer captain David Beckham, notorious for his hairstyles, sported a black cane/cornrow hairstyle. Similarly, Jamaican 'toasting' or DJ-ing (rapping with a mike over instrumental music) while still having a large number of black practitioners/artists has travelled beyond the black community and is a musical form widely used by white and Asian singers, rappers and DJs. Borrowing is a two-way process. Black cultural artisans also import styles and forms from their white, Asian and Chinese peers. Because black culture has travelled beyond the black community and is syn-cretised with other cultural styles and forms some argue that black culture is generally 'hybrid' or mixed today.[5] In recognition of its transcultural nature record producers and musicians coined the term 'urban music' to describe musical forms created amongst African Caribbean, Asian, African and white English youths in the cities and towns of England. So we can't talk about a black culture that belongs exclusively to black people. It is borrowed and consumed across the ethnic spectrum.

A third characteristic of black urban cultures is that they have complex themes and ideas encoded within them. Because culture expresses values, we have to look critically at what is being articulated. Depending upon one's ethical perspective these themes and codes can be viewed as good, bad or neutral. Decoding the values at work in expressive cultures is not an easy task because of divergent views on what is acceptable or reasonable. Hence what may be slack or crude to me may be sweet music to you. It is crucial that when decoding cultural forms we are sensitive towards the context, complexity and genre of a cultural product in order to evaluate its meaning and significance more accurately. For instance, returning to the question of rap and its association with urban violence, it is clear that there is a case to be made against a large quantity of popular large corporate-owned rap music which focuses simply on sex, violence and materialism.[6] However, we must also consider that rappers such as the deceased Tupac Shakur articulate complex socio-political, ethical and cultural ideas in their music and lyrics which are attuned to the commitment for justice in the Civil Rights, Black Panther and black liberation theology movements.[7] From a distance and without proper analysis some rap musical tracks may be perceived as violent and unruly, but more careful consideration may reveal complex and coded articulation of resistance to injustice and poverty. In short, a critical analysis should take place before sweeping statements, such as those by Kim Howells, are thrown into the public arena.

Finally, in the western world today, black cultures are at the centre of popular culture. Whether this refers to street fashion, music or sports, black people in the USA and Britain play a defining role in setting trends. One of the greatest consumers of black music are middle-class white youths in the USA and Britain. The fact that white middle-class suburban youths are a low crime constituency makes Kim Howells' assumption that rap is responsible for violence even less credible.

It could be argued that the dominance of black cultures at school and on the street has led to some black youths selling out to them.[8] What I mean by this is that they are worshipping black cultures and engrossing themselves in the consumption of music and clothing rather than focusing on formal education or more wholesome community-building pursuits. This is the 'gold chains, no brains' argument. I would contend that while black people are at the centre of popular culture, with its potential dangers, we should not ignore the fact they don't own the companies that press the CDs or manufacture the clothes or sports gear. This is an important economic theme that rarely gets the coverage it deserves; black creative genius is still the victim of an organised corporate exploitation in Britain.

Christian Interfaces with Urban Cultures

How then should people of faith engage with urban culture, including what has been termed gun culture? I want to suggest three positions that Christian people may choose to adopt. All of these approaches are based on the presupposition that we are willing to have a critical dialogue with urban cultures. That is to say, that we are not going to ignore it or see it all as 'the work of the Devil'. There are many definitions of dialogue, but what I mean here is a two-way listening process that results in all parties being challenged and changed by the process.

Mission

The first interface that we may choose to have is what I want to call mission. Here the idea is to make relevant the message of the Gospel in the urban cultural context. The purpose is evangelism – to make Christ known in the lives of urban people. It is based on the presupposition that if we can make sure people understand the Gospel message through their cultural lenses then it will be easier to 'make sense' of religion. In order for this to happen we have to locate themes in urban culture that help to explain the liberating message. The message of the Gospel is given priority and urban culture is seen as a tool to help communicate Christ, rather than having a spiritual quality of its own.

Mission works by seeking comparative meanings or practices rather than an idea-for-idea or word-for-word similarity to translate the liberating message of Jesus into a language that gang members understand. For example, I use the word 'dread' in the texts *Jesus is Dread* and *Dread and Pentecostal* to describe the power of Jesus in the world. This translation occurred as a result of seeing how young offenders used the word 'dread' to describe exceptional and sensational occurrences in their lives. Initially I used the phrase 'Jesus is dread' in a prison sermon to describe and translate the life-changing work of Jesus in the world today. 'Dread' became a dynamic equivalent or description of the all-powerful nature of God in Christ. Obviously gang cultures have their own vocabulary and codes and the task of those seeking to evangelise gangs must be like that of the disciples in Acts 1; to communicate in a language that is not their own. To do this you must become familiar with the language by immersing yourself in the culture.

The mission approach, however, is about more than language; it is also about action. Some have used this approach to develop new ways of reaching out to youth in the inner city. For example in January 2003, Les Isaac of the Ascension Trust, a South London evangelistic organisation, developed a 'Street Pastor' outreach in Brixton. Street pastors go out onto the streets and act as negotiators, between minority communities and the police, acting as a calming influence. What Les has done is to translate the beatitudes of peacemaking into a comparative process in the urban context.

The main advantage of the mission approach is that it preserves the essence of the Gospel message. It does not try to dilute it or change it but simply pours it into the cultural context of urban Britain as part of a process of translation.

Recognition

The second way of relating to urban culture is through recognition. This method is concerned with looking to see where God's liberating message and practice are already present in urban cultures. It is based on the presupposition that God is already revealed and at work in contemporary cultures. Whereas the mission interface seeks to pour the Gospel message into the urban context, recognition is concerned with showing that God is already present and at work. The task of Christian people is to uncover this reality, to demonstrate that there is good at work and to identify it as the work of God. This is not a radical departure from the traditional view of God's working in the world. In black Pentecostal circles people believe and sing on Sundays that 'All over the world the Spirit is moving', as an acknowledgement of God's work taking place in the world without the full awareness of those involved in it.

So how is the Spirit of God at work in urban cultures? Wherever we find men and women working for the sake of good, justice and peace we see God's handiwork. As I mentioned above not all forms of black urban cultures are bad. There are cultural artisans who, while not proclaiming to have a faith commitment, have powerful redemptive themes in their work. For example, there are empowering themes in the UK soul music of Beverley Knight and rap artist Ms Dynamite. What I am saying here is that we cannot ignore the fact that in black urban cultures people are searching for meaning, hope and community. Similarly, there are many educational organisations, youth clubs and family welfare groups working in urban environments that seek to empower people, transform relationships and engender hope. When we recognise the divine presence at work in these individuals or organisations we should engage with them and where possible affirm what God is doing in and through them. There are even examples in prison culture where we can discern the presence of God.

This reality became clearer to me when I saw the way that older black men in Birmingham prison would look out for and 'school' new black inmates. These older men would act as father figures. As I saw these relationships develop I was convinced on several occasions that this was one way in which the Spirit of God was at work for the sake of good. On one occasion, I was able to use this example to show an inmate that God was indeed at work in the prison, acting as a protector of the weak and vulnerable. Tragically, in gang cultures dominated by violence the mentoring role has often been used destructively to school criminality rather than to foster wholesome survival skills.

The strength of the recognition approach is that it affirms God's presence in urban cultures. All too often people want to criticise the inner cities and the outer rings as places devoid of goodness or divine activity but this is not the case here. As with the mission approach, recognition makes the starting-point for engagement everyday life, where people are. We should, however, avoid the danger of romanticising urban culture and not taking into account issues of corruption or superficiality. For instance, I once heard a student of mine say that the gangs in our cities were a 'church for youths'. While it is true that there may be some ritual and communal similarities gangs are not qualitatively the same as Christian churches. In short, when we use recognition we must affirm divine presence but also be aware that there is more superficiality than meaningful spirituality at work in urban cultures in Britain today.

Change

The third approach for engaging with urban cultures is working for change. The idea here is to dialogue with the intention of bringing change. The mission approach seeks to get the message across and the recognition approach enables us to discover what God is already doing but the change interface tells us that we achieve nothing unless we change the way things are.

This approach presupposes that Christian engagement with culture is intimately linked to political and economic forces in the world. Put another way, we should not analyse the world without seeking to change it. In recent sociological thought the bringing together of analysis and action has been crystallised in the concept of *praxis*. The word *praxis* describes a way of thinking where thought and action are merged into one. In other words, you 'walk the talk'. If we see that things are wrong, we cannot stand by and let injustice or a particular problem go unchecked. Here, cultural analysis is married to action.

The change approach seeks to be countercultural. That is, it seeks to find new ways of expressing cultural traditions and values that restore hope, engender courage and challenge oppression. It is also an approach that engages in economic analysis of cultural consumption. In short, it aims to get a better deal and appropriate recognition for black cultural artisans.

Far too many urban youths live in and consume cultural forms that are dominated by meaninglessness and hopelessness. Restoring hope is therefore concerned with promoting cultural traditions and values that can inspire and uplift the human spirit in a constructive way. This is not a new idea in British urban contexts. For some time now a plethora of artists, writers, musicians have used their skill to promote a change in outlook amongst young people.

Engendering courage is necessary because of the dominance

of fear. For example, although the relationship between the police and the black community is a complex one, we cannot discount the importance of engendering courage to work with the police in order to rid the streets of criminal gangs and negative cultural influences. Challenging oppression is fundamental to critiquing the media representations of black urban people. As mentioned in the previous chapter, within a postcolonial framework, imagery is one way in which black bodies and minds are controlled and limited in the postcolonial metropolis.

The change approach to exploring culture therefore encourages churches to investigate how they can promote constructive and life-transforming cultural activities that counter the negative images and attitudes towards and of black urban youths. The same approach is relevant when exploring profane lyrics that demean women or encourage the victimisation and attack of gays and lesbians. If every urban church were to set up a media watch group to listen, critique and when needed to complain about oppressive imagery or language, it would go some way towards changing the current negative media approach to representing black life. Likewise, if the National Black Ecumenical organisations were to organise boycotts of newspapers that repeatedly demean black youth this would also be an example of the change approach at work.

In summary, to challenge gang cultures the Church must first understand what culture is and how it works. It must choose methods of engagement that communicate the 'good news of the Gospel' and recognise where and how God is already at work. However, cultural analysis will mean little if it is not accompanied by action, that is challenging the structures that produce problematic images of black, urban life.

Study Questions
- How would you define black urban culture(s)?
- How might your church engage with urban culture(s)?
- How could you/your church engage with gang cultures? What approaches do you consider most appropriate?
- Consider how a media watch group in your church could be

a force for promoting positive images of black people in the media.

- Where do you see God at work in the urban setting today?

Chapter 5

The Place of Blackness
Afrocentric Analysis

Growing up as a youth in the inner city, I was surrounded by negative images and a general ignorance of all things African. Watching Ron Eli portraying the fictional character of 'Tarzan' on British television shaped my earliest impressions of the continent. This Tarzan was a white guy in Africa. He was always shown as the good guy and the black Africans as war-like, savage and stupid. This negative view was affirmed at school. The only mention of Africa in my comprehensive school was when we were fundraising for starving children depicted on Oxfam posters on every corridor. The tragedy of this indoctrination was that during my early teenage years, I denied the African side of my heritage and viewed myself as strictly 'Jamaican' rather than African Caribbean. Twenty years on, there is still a belief amongst sections of the black community that too large a percentage of the third generation of black youths in Britain are 'lost' – estranged from their African roots and heritage. Some would go as far as suggesting that estrangement from one's cultural identity may possibly contribute to nihilistic tendencies manifested in lateral violence (so called black-on-black violence). Basically, a lack of self-knowledge only serves to increase the sense of alienation from oneself and one's community.

When I was growing up in the late 70s and early 80s, this negative outlook was challenged in the reggae music I was listening to at that time. Music by Big Youth, Dennis Brown, Gregory Isaacs, Burning Spear and Steel Pulse was dominated by Rastafarian themes and ideas. Africa in Rastafari is revered as the literal and spiritual homeland of all black people. Consequently,

Africa and African history were unashamedly affirmed, praised and celebrated in this genre. A classic example of reggae's commitment to Africa appears in the music of Bob Marley. Songs such as 'Africa Unite' and 'Zimbabwe' affirm Africa's centrality to all black people.

In contrast, today it is argued that the public politics of reggae and the affirmation of African identity in contemporary black popular music traditions are dead. There has been a retreat in contemporary black popular music from the public sphere into bio-politics, musical forms that focus on personal space, the body, its lusts, poses and posturing.[1] Snoop Dog and 50 Cent are good examples from rap music and Sean Paul and Lady Saw are equivalents from the reggae/dance hall genre. Those who oppose this trend argue that reclamation of African identity is fundamental to a positive self-identity and sense of wellbeing. Such a sense of wellbeing will provide communal context, unity and the collaboration needed for making sense of the systemic failure that surrounds urban youths. For example, the missionary work of the Nation of Islam on the streets of Birmingham and Brixton stresses that a black cultural and political reclamation is needed in order to renew black men and women in Britain. Later, I will stress that urban churches should also develop critical and balanced reclaiming practices.

This chapter will address the benefits of African-centred consciousness as a tool for making sense of and addressing systemic crisis. In short, it will assess how a critical affirmation of blackness, community and solidarity can make a meaningful contribution towards confronting systemic failure. A critical assessment of blackness is necessary because of the problematic role of whiteness in the urban context (as will be shown in chapter 6).

I will begin by describing two perspectives on the nature of black identity in Britain. These are the essentialist and anti-essentialist perspectives. I will then outline the central characteristics of African-centred analysis. I will end by showing how this approach can contribute to urban churches' engagement with systemic failure.

Identity Politics

Firstly, there are those who argue that there is very little if anything of Africa left in the contemporary black experience and we would do well to forget about attempting to reclaim anything African. Our four-hundred-year sojourn in lands far from Africa has removed any meaningful vestiges of Africa in the past. In other words, we are socially, culturally and politically so far removed from Africa that it is ridiculous for black British people to try to reclaim African traditions such as names or religions. There is no mystical or tangible black *essence* uniting black people in one common culture or identity. Instead, the only privileged position held by African Caribbean communities in Britain today is a particular critical stance or perspective that arises from the collision between Africa and Europe in the Caribbean. This position is sometimes called the anti-essentialist view.[2]

A second perspective counters the first argument that there is no common identity, stating that African Caribbean people have retained a great deal of African tradition and culture passed down from slavery to the present. The four-hundred-year exile has not removed African traditions, ideas and values; instead, they have simply been adapted and reshaped by black communities in the Caribbean and Britain. This school will point to aspects of black language, culture and religion in strong and weak forms that have been transported from Africa by its diaspora. African-centred theologians have identified African religious practices and traditions that were transplanted into African Caribbean and African American religious life; voodoo in Haiti could be seen as a prime example. This second school of thought argues that there is a common experience and cultural expectation, or *essence*, which unites black peoples in continental Africa and amongst its diaspora. For this camp, no matter where you are born, if you are black, you are an African.[3]

There is however a third school of thought that occupies a mid point between the essentialist and anti-essentialist schools of thought. This third school acknowledges that links with Africa were damaged but suggests that some traditions were nevertheless passed down in a muted or reshaped fashion to successive generations. This perspective explores the ways that 'Creole' cultures developed in the Caribbean, mixing together or syncretising African and European traditions and cultures to produce a variety of new hybrid cultures. For example, the Caribbean social anthropologist Edward Kamau Brathwaite has pointed out customs, traditions and sayings still in use today amongst contemporary Jamaicans that have their origins in the Creole cultures created by slaves and colonial Jamaicans.[4]

I want to explore African-centred interpretive frameworks, but recognise, as the third approach makes clear, that there are points where our links to the mother country have been weakened, muted and separated. As a result, my definition of Afrocentricity will be a loose one, siding with Stephen Howe's definition of Afrocentricity as:

> an emphasis on shared African origins among all 'black' people, taking pride in those origins and an interest in African history and culture – or those aspects of New World cultures seen as representing African 'survivals' – and a belief that Eurocentric bias has blocked or distorted knowledge of Africans and their cultures.[5]

A 'loose' Afrocentricity, one that recognises that fissures have occurred in black cultures and identities amongst the African diaspora, provides us with a broad framework for affirming commonalities amongst African people, exploring African survivals and challenging the way in which truths about Africans have been distorted in the West. Afrocentric analysis is grounded in a belief that only through an affirmation of African identity, community, economic and social values can black people advance in the face of the current systemic failure.

Afrocentricity

Ironically, much Afrocentric scholarship has taken place, not in Africa but in North America – leading some to deem it sarcastically 'Americocentrism'.[6] This criticism suggests that Afrocentrism must be understood primarily as an African American view of African history and culture. Even so, there is still much to be gained from this perspective and what it has to say to us in the contemporary crisis.

Definition

There is a difference between Afrocentricity and Afrocentrism. The first is an intellectual approach that makes African values, traditions and ideas central to one's thoughts and actions. The second term is associated with ideology that is, unmasking the false ways in which African and African peoples have been represented in European history.[7] Often this second approach has been the matter of great controversy when particular claims are made about the contribution of African people to world civilisation.[8]

How then does Afrocentricity work? What are the chief characteristics of an Afrocentric analysis?

Aims of African-Centred Study

Afrocentric analysis has three aims which can be summarised as follows:
1. To celebrate the achievements of African people and cultures.
2. To analyse how the European worldview has enabled European domination.
3. To construct an alternative framework for understanding and evaluating what it means to be human.[9]

The Celebration of African People and Cultures

Firstly, the celebration of African people and cultures focuses on the roots and routes that have shaped African and African diasporan peoples. This means we not only go back to our roots but also explore the journey or route that has shaped our present reality. This aim assumes that African history and culture are worthy of study and crucial for a fuller understanding of contemporary African diasporan experience.

As mentioned above, there was very little formal study of

Africa within my own school education. Even today, African and Caribbean history is marginal to the mainstream curriculum experienced by most black children. In relation to systemic failure, the celebration motif suggests that making black history, culture and identity central to education and family structures will provide a constructive and wholesome consciousness among black youths. As a social worker told me after the shootings in January 2003, 'These kids need to know who they are. If they valued their blackness they would not do this kind of thing.' Some would argue that studying African history is not of great value because of the immediacy and brutality of the problems we face – how can a study of Africa get the guns off the streets? This is a fair point and no amount of celebration of Africa in classrooms or church halls will substitute for other forms of direct action that need to be taken in the short term. What I do believe is that African history taught within the urban context must be related to the present realities that face black people, in particular the need to transform the social environment and restore hope. For instance, exploring African cultural ideas on community, identity and social struggle could contribute new ideas, values and practices for besieged urban communities today.

There are three areas of caution here that I would like to highlight for consideration. Any meaningful study of Africa must not romanticise the past. We should be critical of our prede-cessors as not everything that was done in the name of African people was good. When exploring African cultures and philo-sophies we should explore how they were 'played out' in everyday life – who benefited and who lost out. For instance, not all African kings and queens ruled justly. So we must be critical of the social values at work in all Ancient African civilis-ations and amongst all dynasties. Likewise, the study of African history must also pay attention to issues of class and gender. It should not simply reproduce the European tradition of focusing on the rich and powerful – the usual kings and queens found in every black history pack. Instead, it should pay attention to roles played by women and men of all class locations. Finally it must consider the economic realities that face continental Africa rather than focussing on the wealth and prosperity of the ancient past.

Analysing the Hegemony of the Eurocentric World View and Ways of Knowing

The second task of Afrocentricity concerns epistemology, that is, how we know that what we know is truthful. An examination of European ways of knowing is important because Afrocentrists seek to expose the whitewashing of African history, culture and values in text books, films and television programmes. Afrocentrists locate the cause of this malaise not in ignorance or mishap but within the very fabric of European thought itself. Put simply, while recognising the diversity of European intellectual traditions, Afrocentrists identify the ways that Western intellectual traditions 'work' to produce neglectful, destructive and deceitful views of Africa and its people. They believe that the problem lies in the Western ways of knowing and being that instinctively marginalise or ignore African alternatives. Therefore to challenge the negative assessment of Africa it is vital that we challenge the way knowledge is collected, assessed and promoted. Take for example, ideas of beauty and intelligence – within both of these categories, African people's contributions have been historically relegated to the margins. As a consequence black supermodels, both male and female, are limited in number and less likely to achieve prestige jobs in Britain.[10] Similarly, at the time of writing black studies are not taught in any major university or college in Britain.

Alternative Frameworks for Understanding

In order to counter the harmful effects of European thought in relation to all things African, people of African descent and others marginalised by a white Western male domination of the structures of thought must construct alternative ways of thinking, being and doing. In other words, Afrocentricity advocates that the best way of empowering black people is to develop our own epistemologies for analysis of the social and political world.

This is not a completely new idea in black history and culture as there are examples in Caribbean history of slaves and colonial subjects placing their own personal experience above and beyond what was being taught at church. So when their master said 'God says, "slaves obey your masters" ', their experience told them that no sensible God sanctioned brutality.[11] Experience as the centre of evaluating knowledge and truth features in more recent attempts to develop alternative ways of knowing for black people. In relation to systemic failure, African-centred thought encourages black people to construct their own ways of evaluating and making sense of the problem. Good examples of Afrocentric analysis in this field are found in the analysis of Pan African and Black Nationalist groupings that seek only solutions that emerge from black experience, culture and civic life.

Afrocentrism and the Urban Church

In order to make use of Afrocentric analysis in the face of systemic failure, the urban Church must first become Afrocentric. There are at least two immediate challenges.

The first challenge is to affirm black history within the Church. Afrocentricity encourages urban churches to celebrate the achievements of black people and address the challenges that face them in an explicit and meaningful way. We should teach African history in every congregation. I have long argued that there is reluctance within many churches to affirm African history and black identity for two reasons, firstly because of an unchecked colonial legacy that informs them that blackness is not really anything to 'rave about', and secondly because of the belief that affirmation would limit the Church's appeal to a diverse constituency. The latter scruple is rather ironic given the fact that fifty years of black ministry in Britain has produced very few diverse congregations.

The kind of affirmation and teaching that is necessary is one that unmasks the negative image of black people in colonial history and attempts to construct a complex and critical understanding of what it means to be black in Britain. Naturally any such celebration cannot be an oppressive practice that marginalises other ethnic groups within the church or community, nor should it ignore the economic realities facing African people today or the responsibilities of the urban Church.[12]

Secondly, African-centred thought encourages urban churches to take seriously the role of Africa in shaping the Christian tradition. How? In black biblical studies the theme of black presence in the Bible has been a central concern for some time. By prioritising African nations, traditions and characters in the Bible scholars seek to demonstrate not only the black presence in Scripture but also its place within the biblical world. This view is exemplified in Dr Randall Bailey's analysis of Africans and African nations in *Stony the Road We Trod: African American Biblical Interpretation* (1991).[13] Consider Bailey's reading of the narrative of the Queen of Sheba (1 Kings 10). Here, Bailey argues that the Queen of Sheba as an African woman is the one who *appraises* Solomon's wisdom, thus demonstrating the importance of African intellectual thought in the ancient world:

> As one looks at the narrative it appears that there are several keys to the question of valuation. Firstly, the fact that the writer is trying to establish, or further ground, Solomon as the one who is wise. The vehicle used is that of having him pass the test of African riddles and wisdom. The assumption, therefore, of the narrator is that this is the most difficult test to be posed. The African Queen states: 'The report was true which I heard in my own land of your affairs and of your wisdom, but I did not believe the reports until I came and my own eyes had seen it; and behold, the half was not told to me; your wisdom and prosperity surpass the report which I heard' (vv. 6–7).[14]

In summary, there are a variety of perspectives on to what degree black people retain African traditions today. I have proposed a loose Afrocentrism as a resource for affirming black history in both secular and religious contexts. However, I have raised numerous questions about the approach to an African-centred analysis, primarily that it cannot descend into a romanticised practice that values everything African or black.

Afrocentrism offers a specific communal experience as a focus for action and empowerment. The task for the urban Church is to embrace the best of Afrocentricity in a quest for balanced, affirmed and empowered black identities both inside and outside the Church. A good introductory book is *Afrocentric Sermons: The Beauty of Blackness in the Bible* by Kenneth L. Walters (USA: Judson Press, 1993).

Study Questions
- What experience of Africa have you had at home and school? How does it compare with mine?
- What is the essentialist position? What is the anti-essentialist position? Which do you find most appealing? Why?
- What is Afrocentrism? How does it differ from Afrocentricity?
- What is the aim of African-centred study?
- Should black history be taught in urban churches? Why/why not?
- If you were to set up a programme of black history reading in your church, which elements would be included? Why?

Chapter 6

What Does It Mean to Be White?

Understanding Whiteness in the Urban Context

A little over a week after the January shootings in 2003, one of Birmingham's coroners inflamed the situation by making derogatory remarks regarding the African Caribbean community's place within the city. Speaking at the inquest of one of the victims he said that it was time for black people to 'pay back' efforts to accommodate them in a multicultural society. He then went on to say to black people that 'your community' should 'conform with our belief' that it was every citizen's duty to co-operate with the police. He ended his tirade with a plea for harmony as, 'Birmingham prides itself on being a multiracial city and the authorities go to great lengths to accommodate all the different cultures.'[1] Naturally, the Home Secretary and a plethora of community and police leaders denounced his comments. Eventually Mr Cotter apologised, stating that his remarks were not intended to cause offence.

This event revealed not only that colonial images of black people were still present, but also that that the coroner did not have an understanding of how issues of race and power are played out in the city. The white leadership within the city has constructed a vision of multiculturalism that excludes and makes invisible the workings of white people, as 'multicultural' refers to everyone who is not white. The fact that after fifty years of visible black presence very few white people have had to think critically on being white is related to the experience and history of black people in the city. Given the problem of the lack of critical awareness of whiteness amongst white people, this chapter is geared towards assisting white urban Christians to reassess their role in the struggle against systemic failure.

Speaking personally, the question of what it means to be white never bothered me until recently. I'd spent most of my working life exploring the ways in which black experience, identity and culture(s) behave and had very little time for examining what it meant to be white or the concept of whiteness. But this was a mistake.

Frantz Fanon, one of the most important anticolonial writers of the mid twentieth century, discovered that both colonised people and colonisers are damaged by the experience of oppression. Through his work as a psychiatrist in Algeria during the country's war of independence, he diagnosed mental illnesses among the French colonialists that were the consequence of the colonial war.[2]

What I am registering here is the fact that we have not yet got to grips with how three centuries of British colonialism, imperialism and racism have had a negative impact upon what it means to be white and British, and created a psychological and political fallout. This is an important yet neglected area of evaluation for white Christians in the urban context. Even the most recent media exploration of Empire on Channel 4 (Niall Ferguson's *Empire: How Britain Made the Modern World*, 2003), failed to get to grips with the social, psychological and cultural impact of the British Empire on white British people. Instead, that particular series ended with the usual celebration of multiculturalism in Britain.

I am proposing that in order to work for justice in the urban context, it is necessary to understand whiteness. Systemic failure is also related to issues of racism and the Apartheid-like geography and power dynamics of many urban contexts in Britain. For churches working for change it is necessary to understand what constitutes whiteness, or, to parody W. E. B. Du Bois, the souls of white folk. In this chapter we will begin with a definition of whiteness and some of its characteristics, and go on to explore how studying and understanding whiteness can contribute to the struggle against systemic failure.

Understanding Whiteness

Whiteness is difficult to define because its essential meaning will vary from context to context and from situation to situation. When most of us think about whiteness, we refer to skin colour. But whiteness is about more than just the epidermis; it is also about behavioural characteristics, social location and worldview. Ironically, many black urban cultures have created urban myths about whiteness that hint at a perceived superior intellectual and moral character. During talks I have given in inner city schools on the virtues of higher education, I've heard black kids in school use the phrase 'acting white' to describe performing well at school or playing what are perceived as élitist sports such as polo or croquet! Similarly, I've listened to conversations where whiteness is associated with correct moral behaviour as expressed in the phrase 'act the white man'.

What I am suggesting here is that whiteness is the way in which ideas, myths and language are used to ensure that white skin colour is represented in a particular, superior way. Now, we know that not all white people are the same and that issues of ethnicity, class, gender and even sexuality impact upon how one is treated. Decades of feminist scholarship have made clear that gender plays a role in the workplace, the home and the Church. White men and white women do not always have the same social standing. Similarly, the recent negative experience of some Eastern European refugees in inner cities informs us that class and nationality also distinguish white people.

I often joke with white asylum seekers I have befriended that if they play their cards right, within a generation they will become fully white! What I mean by this is that whiteness as a form of social advantage is not a closed door, as you can become white or gain admittance to the club. This is also true for a select group of black people. No one would doubt that General Colin Powell, who at the time of writing is the US Secretary of State, has ascended to the lofty heights of white privilege in America.

What then are some of the characteristics of whiteness in the contemporary urban situation? How does whiteness work?

Invisibility

The first point to note about whiteness is that it is an invisible norm. We tend not to see it as part of the cultural mix. This is why the coroner was able to present multiculturalism in Birmingham as a collection of Asian and African Caribbean communities. We don't generally place white people (whether English, Irish, Welsh or Scottish) within the multicultural mix. Consequently, multi- or intercultural issues are often seen as the preserve and concern only of non-whites.

Because whiteness is unmarked racially, some white people tend not to see it in operation in everyday life. For example, when I ask my predominantly white undergraduate students to tell me five things about being white, they freeze and have no answers. In contrast, if I ask my predominantly black group of postgraduates they are full of suggestions! Those looking in from the outside seem to be more aware of the issues than those on the inside. However, it is also evident that white students who have lived in minority white situations tend to be more aware of debates and issues concerning being white.

There is an important point to be made here; because whiteness and white people are not 'racialised' in the same way as other groups, whiteness is able to function as an ethnically neutral category that can go unexplored and unchallenged as the standard for expectation and evaluation. As mentioned in the discussions on Afrocentricity, white standards of intelligence and beauty are still invisible norms that operate in contemporary culture and politics. For many black people in Britain today, to be accepted as 'normal' in white dominated circles of power and influence requires a sacrifice of aspects of black identity and culture.[3]

Economic Advantage

As well as being invisible, whiteness is also a place or location associated with privilege. In the summer of 2002, the BBC screened a documentary entitled *Trading Races*. For this series a black African Caribbean man and a white English woman and man were cosmetically transformed to take on the features of another ethnic group. Morphed into a white person, the black man was able to march with the far right British National Party and also attend dog races – two activities that he would never have been able to participate in as himself. It was interesting to note that, time and time again, the black man expressed how differently people treated him when he appeared as a white man, showing that even in working-class settings, such as a greyhound track, being white had certain advantages.

Tragically, in the real world, whiteness as a structural advantage is played out to the detriment of black people in our nation's classrooms, employment statistics, promotional opportunities and health provision. Whiteness is for most white people a place of economic advantage, even in an age of equal opportunities and community cohesion.[4]

Discourse(s)

The most interesting aspect of whiteness for me is that it gains strength by drawing from other discourses or particular representations of bodies of knowledge. A good and relevant example of this process for us as Christians is the way in which whiteness is still synonymous in Western theology with goodness and the presence of the divine. God is still thought of as an old white man and Jesus depicted as an Aryan in most city churches. The repercussions of this logic have a public expression; in civic life it becomes natural to associate whiteness with correct moral behaviour and blackness with deviance. As a black professional, I experience the negative outcome of the interface between whiteness and intelligence on most occasions when, away from the university, I have to present or introduce myself by my professional title. On one occasion a secretary working for the BBC came looking for me in the lobby of a BBC building in London. I sat in my suit waiting next to a white motorcycle courier who was clad in black leathers. There were only two of us waiting in the lobby. Intriguingly, the secretary approached the cyclist next to me and asked, 'Are you Dr Beckford?'

Terror

When discussing whiteness we cannot forget that for many people in the urban context whiteness is still is associated with racial terror. There is a perception that when senior white politicians make negative statements about the ethnicity of black people, for example when commenting on crime or asylum, the lives of minority ethnic people are put in real danger. The steady rise of racial attacks and the failure to eliminate discrimination against black people clearly shows that racial terror is still a feature of contemporary British life.[5]

Appropriation

Another dimension of whiteness is the way in which it is put together or constructed through an appropriation of aspects of other cultures.[6] This is particularly visible in youth culture in Birmingham and other towns and cities in Britain. As I walk through the library area of Birmingham on Saturday afternoons, I am confronted with young white kids wearing clothing originating within black urban cultures of the Caribbean and North America. This cultural borrowing is not new; those old enough to remember the 1960s or 1970s 'mods' will remember that in both incarnations this youth culture was deeply associated with the soul music and style of inner city Detroit, New York and Chicago. For some time now, white youths have borrowed black style and language, but as mentioned above, often, credit and material reward for black cultural innovation is not given to the black community.

Antiracism

Finally, I believe that whiteness is at its most significant when it is associated with antiracism. There has been a long if often hidden tradition of whiteness being a part of a symbol of the struggle for justice. Sadly, even our churches have not fully recognised and celebrated white men and women who fought to free slaves, marched against fascists in the East End of London, stood in solidarity with Gandhi or marched with Dr Martin Luther King.

My first awakening to this reality of whiteness was during the 1970s when the anti-Nazi league marched through Birmingham city centre. My family were in town to shop, and as we drove through the Digbeth region of Birmingham, where the protest was taking place, I was amazed and intrigued by the fact that 99 per cent of the marchers were white. A second occurred during my secondary school years. The teachers who had the greatest influence on my academic development were white radicals committed to the intellectual advancement of black children. What distinguished Ms Jewell, Ms Delgarno, Mr Brown, Andy Wright and Mr Ralph was their ability to politicise the educational process, so that black children such as myself became conscious of the relationship between education and black empowerment.

A third awakening occurred during my first teaching post at a theological seminary in the West Midlands. During six interesting years of teaching trainee Anglican and Methodist clergy, I was deeply impressed by one of my colleagues, John Wilkinson, an Anglican priest who demonstrated through his life and ministry a radical commitment to racial justice. He had developed a theology and practice that reconstructed white, Christian identity so that it took on an inclusive, dynamic and progressive quality.

Despite these examples of good practice black professionals know all too well that there is a capacity within whiteness discourse to have the language and appearance of racial justice but to lack the practical application and substance. The above awakenings were significant because they demonstrated that there were places and spaces where whiteness had gone beyond a superficial inclusion and demonstrated practical commitment.

In short, whiteness is a complex concept to describe and define and not every white person will fit neatly into the categories I have just outlined. Neither will every white person be comfortable with whiteness being talked about. Even today, whiteness is still intimately related to social, economic and political power. Its power is maintained in part by whiteness's intersection with other discourses such as beauty and intelligence. However, in contrast, there are also traditions and visions of whiteness within the urban context that are inclusive and entwined with the struggle for racial justice.

What I want to suggest in the remainder of this chapter is that unless we are willing to talk about and address what whiteness means in the world, we will never get to grips with how it has functioned in a destructive way for everyone, and in particular for white people.

Doing White Studies

Making sense of whiteness is vitally important because without a serious discussion of this subject, we leave a free space for the right wing in the Labour and Conservative Parties and the extreme parties such as the right-wing British National Party to exploit the hearts and minds of vulnerable and ill-informed whites, and to be the only voices articulating what it means to be white and British in the urban context today. There can be no meaningful discussion of urban issues that concern race and ethnicity if the only white contributions are from those who have redeemed their whiteness – what cultural theorist Les Back calls, 'stepping out of whiteness'.[7] This is particularly important for white Christian contributions to the discussion on gun crime gang violence. To this end several tools are required.

Firstly, there is a need to engage in historical analysis. We need to know where, when and why whiteness came into being. Also, we need to look at how it has been deployed in the urban context in British history, particularly in relation to African and Asian people. Systemic failure is in part the product of racialised oppression produced by an unchecked, subtle yet brutal white-ness. Such an exploration must always consider issues of class, economics and gender in order to unlock the various levels of experience in white British history.

Secondly, it is important to examine how racism works in the world of business and the workplace as well as in social settings, since systemic failure is intimately related to issues of race in the educational, criminal justice and welfare systems. It is crucial that white people become conscious of the hidden workings of whiteness in order to produce new ways of thinking about white identities and cultures. It should also produce a new discourse inspired by unearthing hidden ways of thinking and being white.

The psychological cost and damage of whiteness must also be evaluated in any meaningful study. The purpose should be to critique the idea that being white and gaining entrance to the 'club' is painless.[8]

Finally, any church engaging in critical white study must explore the ways in which Christian thought has been bound up with the worse excesses of whiteness. Unfortunately at the time of writing there exists no credible group of British-based Christian scholars dedicated to unmasking and weakening the hold of racist discourse on Christian theology. Creating resources is therefore a priority for those seeking to rethink the presentation of the Christian gospel in a multicultural context.

In summary, one of the major aims of a meaningful and critical approach to whiteness is to ensure that white Christians in white majority churches in the urban context take responsibility for racism that has an impact on systemic failure. This means not just seeing racism as a black issue but as something that all churches have to be actively engaged in struggling against. This task requires a commitment to exploring the discourse on white-ness and where necessary reconstructing whiteness so that it is more able to make a meaningful contribution to the fight against systemic failure.

Study Questions

- Do you agree with Fanon's findings about the cost of racism for white people?

- Why does whiteness appear to be invisible to many white people?
- How does white skin secure privilege? Is this always a hard and fast rule?
- How does whiteness draw on other discourses?
- In what ways was the author awakened to the antiracist dimensions of whiteness? Have you had similar experiences/ insight?
- What tools are needed to do critical white studies? What should be some of the aims of a study of whiteness?
- How might you incorporate a critical approach to whiteness into your teaching, ministry or church life?

SECTION 3

Biblical Reflection

Chapter 7

The Politics of Interpretation

In section 2 we explored a selection of socio-cultural frameworks that offer a particular interpretation of the systemic failure that produces gun crime and gang violence. As mentioned in the introduction, these are specific and related to my belief that certain cultural and sociological tools are more useful and accessible for urban churches than others.

This section has four chapters. In the first, we examine the politics of interpretation, the nuts and bolts of how and where interpretation takes place. The second and third chapters examine two radical interpretive methods that best draw out themes, models and ideas that address systemic failure. The final chapter is an illustration of how to interpret Scripture using the interpretive methods. The aim of the section is to provide a new way of reading and interpreting Scripture so that it more effectively addresses the specific social, cultural and political context that I have associated with systemic failure. We begin with the politics of interpretation.

At almost every Sunday service in many of the churches that I have worshipped in, I have heard the preacher say, just before the sermon, that they have a message for the congregation that 'God has laid on their heart'. This statement suggests that God, through the Holy Spirit, has guided the preacher to a particular passage of Scripture and given them a unique and specific interpretation for that congregation. Within this scheme, interpretation is understood to be a highly spiritual process where paragraphs of the Bible are lifted and placed into the present world to illuminate or rebuke the believers under the supernatural inspiration of the Spirit. So one can only interpret properly if one 'has the Spirit'.

Having spent most of my life in black Pentecostal churches, I have also noticed that interpretation is generally a case of finding like-for-like correspondences between a story, principal or theme in the Bible and the contemporary situation facing the congregation. Here the Bible functions as a book of guidelines providing all the information needed to live well in the world. Using this approach to interpretation, if we are struggling with our financial situation, we find a passage that on the surface appears to deal with money and copy the principles expanded within it.

In this chapter, I want to argue that this particular approach, based on the illuminating power of the Spirit and the information on the pages of the Bible, is limited in relation to our concern to speak prophetically into the crisis that faces us. In order to ensure that Scripture constructively informs thinking and action, we must first begin by considering what is meant by biblical interpretation and where and how interpretation takes place. I will contend that by focusing on the dialogue between the socio-political world of the reader and that of the text, we are more likely to identify readings that illuminate our understanding and response to systemic failure.

Interpretation

The word used in Christian theology to refer to the process of interpretation is hermeneutics. The origin of this word is found in Greek mythology; the god Hermes carried the messages of the gods to humans. This role included the act of translation. Hermeneutics then, is the overall process of interpreting the meaning of events.

The interpretation of biblical texts has always formed a considerable part of Christian theology. But, during the Renaissance in Western Europe, hermeneutics emerged as a touchstone because of its importance in defending the relative positions of Catholic and Protestant traditions. In modern theological thought, hermeneutics has become a science and an art. So what does it mean to talk about interpretation today? I want to explore it as the dynamic interplay between the world of the reader and the world of the biblical text.

Fig. 2

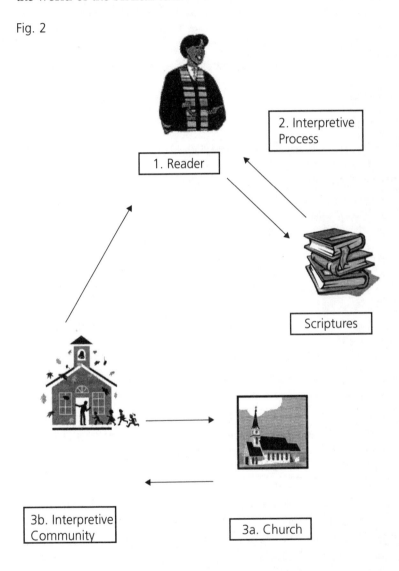

Factors Influencing Interpretation

The best way to explore this interplay is to first identify the factors involved in interpreting a portion of Scripture. Interpretation does not occur in a vacuum. When preachers get up to preach, under the inspiration of the Spirit, they are also influenced by other factors that may not be evident to their hearers. There are at least three major influences on the act of interpretation in urban churches. These are the reader's bias, the interpretive process and communities of influence. Let's begin with the reader's bias.

The Reader

A first location influencing interpretation is the personal experience of the reader (fig. 2, no. 1) – the one doing the interpreting. Everyone who approaches the biblical text has biases, concerns and other subjective perspectives that they bring to the Bible every time they read it. In other words, we approach the Scriptures with pre-understanding or bias. These pre-understandings, if unchecked, can be projected onto the Bible so that the interests of the reader are subconsciously read into the Bible.[1]

This is not a new theme in the history of black African and Caribbean people. We know that racism as a subjective pre-understanding among plantation owners was projected onto Bible texts in order to justify slavery.[2] Womanist (black feminist) scholars have demonstrated the ways that male bias or patriarchy has also influenced the interpretation of the Bible.[3] There are many examples from the history of Christianity where men have been keen to emphasise Scriptures that limit the participation of women in the community and church and ignore Scriptures that emphasise women doing the will and work of God. For instance, in the Wesleyan Holiness Church tradition in which I was raised, strict dress codes were deployed in order to monitor and control the role of women in the church at the expense of more liberating readings that identified women participating in the ministry of Jesus and the building of the first churches in the Acts. Scriptures such as 1 Corinthians 11:5–6, which instructs women to cover their heads while preaching and prophesying, were used to ensure that women covered their heads in church at all times. Even though it was clear that a hat did not limit the measure of God's Spirit at work in the life of an individual, the cultural biases of the older Caribbean men in leadership ensured that this rule was enforced, and a woman caught not wearing a hat was subject to the discipline of the denomination.

According to this perspective on how reading takes place, interpretation does not occur on the pages of the Bible but instead in the life of the reader. How the reader understands him- or herself is crucial, because self-understanding has an impact on the interpretation of the text. For example, if we read the Bible in the traditional spiritual way, believing that God will speak to us supernaturally and that the text is to be understood in an objective way, then our interpretation will be 'spiritualised'. Alternatively, if we read the Bible fully aware of the social, political and cultural issues that inform our self-understanding (postcolonialism, cultural context, whiteness and Afrocentric awareness), our interpretation will be more likely to have a socio-political and cultural orientation. The second influence is the interpretive process.

Interpretive Process

A second location suggests the opposite, namely that the centre of interpretation is found within the interpretive process (fig. 2, no. 2) itself rather than within the life of the reader. The inter-pretive process is the dialogue between a reader and the Scripture. For example, sometimes when I read the Bible, I find myself having an internal discussion in my own mind about the passage and wrestling with its meaning and significance. Occasionally when we approach the Bible we find that it provides more questions than answers: at this point it is suggested by biblical interpreters that 'the Bible interprets us', because we are forced to reconsider our pre-understandings. Some suggest that because of this interplay it is not evident whether the text or the reader dominates in this approach.[4]

As mentioned above, within urban church circles, reader–text dialogue is primarily a Spirit-inspired process where the Spirit leads the reader into a deeper understanding of the text. Many urban churches solve the text–reader domination question by collapsing reader and text into one interpretive voice achieved 'through the Spirit', making the reader and text indivisible. As we shall see later, this second context requires particular tools to unlock what the Bible has to say in our contemporary situation.

Interpretive Communities

Finally, even though readers read and are part of an interpretive dialogue, the big picture also influences them. What I mean by this is that the Church's traditions and other social communities influence how we interpret the Bible.[5]

In the case of the Church (fig. 2, no. 3a), we are influenced by the doctrines that we sign up to when we become members of a church. Sometimes we adhere to them even if they don't make sense in the real world. For example, for a long time one of the major black majority churches, the Church of God of Prophecy, insisted that all of its members who were married did not wear wedding rings. This was because they believed that the Bible did not permit the wearing of jewellery, even wedding rings. Many sensible, intelligent people within this denomination adhered to this rule despite at times being unsure of its intellectual soundness. So sometimes we read and interpret the Bible under the influence of the ethical sensibilities of church doctrine.

We are also influenced by other social groupings. In my case the theological, or interpretive community (fig. 3, no. 3b) also influences how I read and interpret the Bible. Being influenced by scholarly approaches to the Bible informs my pre-understanding. However, being part of the Caribbean diaspora also has an impact on how I read and interpret. Raised in a Caribbean household, I was taught never to forget the value of my church education despite my academic learning. Through experience and absorption of cultural traditions, I was provided with alternative ways of validating the truthfulness of a statement or idea. For instance, despite being taught in the academy by New Testament scholars that supernatural miracles do not happen, I still believe in God's supernatural power to heal and transform. This is because the world-view passed down from my Caribbean Christian ancestors has a greater impact on how I interpret and understand the supernatural in the world today.

In short, we never read as neutrals. Our own pre-understand-ings and the influence of church doctrine and other significant communities always affects us in some way. If we are aware of our biases we are better able to distinguish between the voice of God, culture and personal prejudice.

Now that we have explored some of the factors influencing interpretation, our next task is to identify how interpretation takes place. A good way of exploring this theme is to look at the places where interpretation occurs.

Locations in which Interpretation Occurs

Fig. 3

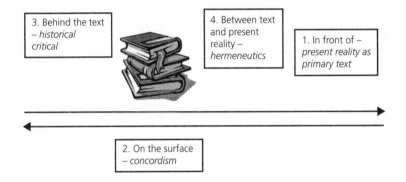

Liberation theologian J. S. Croatto has suggested five approaches to interpretation.[6] Four are useful to our study of where interpre-tation takes place.

The first location (fig. 3, no. 1) is termed *present reality as primary text*. Here interpretation takes place in the world in which we live. We don't go to the Bible but just work out what God is saying from reading the 'signs of the times' presented in the world around us. This approach is built on the belief that God speaks through world events and personal circumstances. For example, on many occasions, Christian people see an event take place in their lives and interpret it as a sign from God. In this way, the present reality functions as a 'text' or living scripture to be interpreted by the believer. The strength of this approach is that we learn to see God's action in the world. The weakness is that we may be tempted to dispense with Scripture altogether and just concentrate on the social context, failing to see the connectedness between the two.

The second position (fig. 3, no. 2), *concordism*, refers to a surface reading of the Bible. Whereas the first position places the theological locus or centre in front of the text, so as to interpret real life events as God's word at work in the world today; this position explores the surface of the text itself. Here meaning is found on the pages of the Bible where the acts of God are recorded. Interpretation is simply a like-for-like translation of texts. As mentioned above, this is still the approach to interpretation adopted by most urban churches in Britain. Concordism can have powerful affects. For example, I once heard a member of a church speak of a time when he was once contemplating suicide. He opened the window of his flat, ready to jump out. Halfway out of the window he saw a copy of the Bible on a shelf. He said aloud to God, 'If you are real speak to me through the first thing I read in the Bible.' He turned to Genesis 1:1, and the first word he read was 'in'. He took this as a sign to close the window and abort the suicide attempt. Although in this particular case the interpretation led to a positive outcome, this approach can be limited because it fails to explore the historical context, nuance or genre of a text and rigidly believes that what is read in the pages of the Bible is its meaning.[7]

A third approach (fig. 3, no. 3), *historico-critical methods*, defines modern biblical analyses that explore the historical and cultural background of a text in order to identify genres and codes that inform its construction. Here, the privileged theological locus is behind the text, wrapped up in historical archaeology. This approach takes seriously the historical study of the Bible and its languages and also analyses where and how Scripture was put together. There are many benefits to be gained from this approach because it provides us with facts and data about Scripture, which inform us of the world in which the text was written and enable us to make better sense of what was recorded. Despite the numerous benefits to be gained from this method, its main downfall is that it focuses almost exclusively on what happened behind the text and is separated from what goes on in front of it in the modern world.[8]

The final approach that I want to explore is *hermeneutics*. Hermeneutics places the focus of interpretation on the world of the reader and the world of the text. It is in this interplay or dialogue between present reality and the text where interpretation takes place. As mentioned above, readers never read alone. So this interplay is part of a wider circle of interpretation.

Put simply hermeneutics, as it is used here, does not mean that we avoid what lies behind the text, the historical archaeology; instead we recognise that there is history behind the Bible. This enables us to avoid the dangers of reading the surface of the text, which is of vital importance when considering the ethnic origins of nations and individuals in the Bible. A more informed ethnology would enable us to see the rich multicultural and multi-ethnic world in which biblical events occur. For people of the African diaspora in particular, broader background awareness would identify the host of African nations and individuals who play a progressive role in God's plan of salvation. For some time now black biblical scholars such as Charles Copher, Cain Hope Felder and Randall Bailey have encouraged black communities to read and interpret the Bible in awareness of biblical ethnography.[9]

Even being aware of the biblical languages of Hebrew and Greek can help to explain the background and meaning of text more fully. I once heard of a Christian sect in America who interpreted, 1 John 4:4 'whatsover is born of God overcometh the world' (KJV) as a literal statement that salvation led to perfection of the individual Christian on earth. If the sect had paid attention to the tense of the sentence, they would have noted that it is present active and therefore describing a continual struggle and an overcoming, not an arrived at state of perfection. For a practical example of how this hermeneutical approach is applied see chapter 10 where I reread Exodus 1 in the light of gun crime and gang violence.

In Search of an Urban Political Reader's Interpretive Ethic

To recap, interpretation as understood here is the reciprocal dialogue between the socio-political worlds of the reader and Scripture. In concluding this chapter, I want to explore in brief some of the steps involved in this process of dialogue.

Firstly, the dialogue must be guided by a search for the liberation ethic within the text. I am referring to awareness of the trajectory of a particular issue or theme. There are times when what appears on the surface to be oppressive is liberating within its historical context. For example, when Paul tells Philemon to take back his slave, not as a slave but as a 'brother' (Philemon 1) we see an attempt to move beyond the limitations of the historical context (Greco-Roman slavery) and provide a new model of relationship between those enslaved and those who are free. When brought into our context, this text affirms the human dignity of all people and a Christian commitment to remove all barriers, whether physical or spiritual, that limit individual and communal wellbeing.

There are times when the values we have today are actually better than those at work in parts of the Bible. There are disturbing and degrading images of women and stories of genocidal brutality which centuries of Christian ethics have taught us to dismiss. When faced with this reality, we must acknowledge that God's presence in our present reality takes priority in the interpretation. For example, scholars have pointed out a negative imagery of Canaanites in Old Testament Israelite thought that cannot be condoned.[10] The negative 'othering' presenting others as opposite to yourself (in this case presenting the Canaanites as intellectual, sexual and physical inferiors) warns us of the danger of demonising groups today. Verbal and visual 'othering' has provided a framework for much brutality in the past and present.

Finally, we must expect Scripture to challenge us. There are times when the text speaks prophetically and critically into our life setting. As will be demonstrated in chapter 10, the work of the midwives in Exodus 1 challenges us to become their equivalents today working to save our male children from a social situation that seeks to limit their life possibilities.

In summary, there are a variety of factors that influence the art of interpretation. The reader, the interpretive process and social context all bear upon how interpretation occurs. The interpretive process itself considers what happens behind, in front of and on the surface of the text. I have recommended an approach to interpretation that prioritises the ongoing dialogue between the world of the text and the world of the reader. Interpretation seeks out the liberative ethic within the text and expects Scripture to challenge our ways of thinking and doing today.

Study Questions
- What is meant by the term hermeneutics?
- What are the three factors influencing the process of interpretation? What approach to reading/interpreting Scripture do you adopt? Why?
- How effective is the form of interpretation used at your church in responding to gun crime and gang violence?
- What is the liberation ethic? Can you cite examples from Scripture?
- Can we take a critical approach to interpretation and still claim to be guided by the Spirit of God? Or are the two processes mutually exclusive?

Chapter 8

Me, My Text and I

Reader–Response Interpretation

In this chapter, I want to present the first of two strategies for interpreting the Bible that enable the reader to hold fast to the issues and concerns that arise from analysis of a social location blighted by systemic failure. For many people within the urban context there exists a conflict between doing critical analysis and being part of a worshipping community. This is usually known as the 'leaving your brains at the church door' syndrome. You can work all week in an urban context defined by issues of racism, sexism or social exclusion, but on Sunday morning you are expected to leave these issues at the door. Here I want to combine faith in the power of the Spirit to transform the world with social analysis in order to interpret the Bible afresh, anew and in a way that is relevant to systemic failure. There are a variety of approaches that we can explore, but I want to outline two that have been most helpful in my teaching in the academy, the Church and also with black men in prisons. The first is reader-response interpretation.

Reader Response

There is no one set version of reader-response interpretation as it comprises various schools of thought with their own particular methods.[1] As mentioned in the previous chapter, one area in which meaning can occur is in the world of the reader. Readers are not objective. Every reader has biases and I have suggested that these biases if unchecked can also go unquestioned as we interpret Scripture. Reader-response interpretation affirms the centrality of the reader in the process of interpretation and it is here that meaning is found.

In its simplest form, reader-response interpretation argues that in order to discover the meaning of a passage, the reader must explore the Scriptures in response to their own situation, in an explicit way. In this sense, meaning and significance is the product of the dialogue between the world of the reader and the world of the text. This is not a completely new idea in urban churches. For nearly half a century congregations have read the Bible mindful of the spiritual needs of migrant communities from the Caribbean and Africa. From my perspective, what is new is that we make explicit in our reading of the Bible the political, cultural and social issues that now confront us. Later, I will describe this reading perspective as an urban socio-political reading.

The strength of reader-response approaches for interpretation is that they place a real emphasis upon the everyday experiences of ordinary people. They enable us to bring to the Bible every care, concern and issue and to search for meaning in the world in which we live. However, there are dangers. Reader response must be part of a broader reading convention or framework (as demonstrated previously) so that a person has the opportunity to check their interpretations against the input from the Church, academy and community. If this checking process does not happen then it increases the risk of errant interpretations based on an unchallenged subjectivity. History is full of individuals and groups who arrived at strange doctrines because they read in complete isolation and with no regard to what was happening around them or what had gone before.

Reader Response in Urban Churches

I grew up in a black church where reader response was encouraged but only on a spiritual level. In other words, we interpreted the text in terms of its meaning for our 'spiritual being' rather than our 'earthly, postcolonial, Afrocentric, cultural being'. So if we read a passage about justice for oppressed people in the Old Testament, we spiritualised the passage so that the justice theme was interpreted as a 'spiritual justice' or God's hidden work, in the world, in which we played little part. Consequently, we failed to make a connection between the social and political realities of Scripture and those of our world.

This limited form of reader response in many urban churches can often be a communal experience. People read the Bible together and interpret its meaning in cell groups or Bible study groups. Communal readings are useful checks and balances against errant or bogus interpretations. However, when read in community, interpretation is subject to all the pre-understandings and traditions of that community. Sometimes this means that any new interpretations will be viewed with caution or suspicion. However, in an open and exploratory environment new readings may be highly prized and affirmed.

Also, reader response in urban churches, and particularly in Pentecostal or Charismatic churches, are grounded in a strong belief in the guidance of the Holy Spirit.[2] Put simply, people believe that the Spirit is guiding them as they interpret. I believe the work of the Spirit in the world is liberation – to free men and women from every force, system or structure that prevents them from embracing God's transformative power – but the Spirit's guidance in interpretation can be a problematic process if the interpreter does not distinguish between their own biases and the impetus of the Spirit.

Finally, in many urban churches, particularly black Pentecostal ones, reading and action are interwoven. If you interpret a passage it is not to stay in your head, but to become a part of your life. In this sense the Bible becomes a powerful book, where right interpretation transforms lives and propels people into action.

Towards an Urban Socio-political Reader

As mentioned at the beginning of the previous chapter, one of the stumbling blocks to a more relevant and grounded approach to interpretation is the singular use of the 'spiritualised approach'.

Within the spiritualised approach the reader's self-under-standing is that of a disembodied spiritual being with no social, economic, cultural or political perspective or context to influence the interpretive process. In response, what I want to offer here is an approach to interpretation that makes connections between the socio-political concerns of the reader and similar concerns within the Bible. This approach prioritises the cultural, social and political factors that influence the reader. In this case, the experiences and structures that impact upon systemic failure and our analysis of the situation are at the forefront as we approach a passage for interpretation. The aim is to draw out of the text parallel issues that can challenge the social world in which we inhabit. Put simply, if I am concerned about systemic failure and outlaw culture, then I have to bring these issues to the text.

For example, taking our experience and analysis of living in postcolonial circumstances and bringing that to the text trans-forms our perspective on the colonial narratives in the Old Testament such as the Hebrew bondage in Egypt and Babylon. Moreover, Jesus' teachings take on a new dimension, as we become aware that he was, on one level, a colonised Jew suffering economic and political oppression. From this vantage point, Jesus' teachings take on a new quality for those living under neocolonial conditions in Britain.

Our cultural considerations can also be brought to the Scrip-tures. We can ask of the Bible questions such as 'How can cultural forms be fashioned so that they reflect the love and power of God working for justice in the world?' To this end we should reassess how Jesus evaluates what is meaningful and engages with the cultural traditions of his day, seeking to discover Jesus' cultural hermeneutic, that is, how he interprets culture. We may also want to address how cultural traditions are demonised. Why and how are certain groups' cultural systems the basis of marginalisation? This question will provide new opportunities to identify with those in Scripture who find themselves on the receiving end of negative cultural imagery. For example, in the conquest narratives of the Old Testament the representation of Canaanites by Israel are often similar to those used by colonial powers to demean and conquer Africans.[3]

Similarly, the social quest for the recognition and affirmation of black identities as found in Afrocentrism are brought to bear on Scripture. Not only do we seek to identify with the black presence in the Bible, but also to explore the complex and varied ways in which black people and African nations are represented in Scripture.

Finally, reader response enables us to consider the behavioural motivations that foster criminal activity. We are able to explore texts that identify the ways that bad intentions fester and develop in human hearts. Jesus' teachings of how bad intentions are formed in the heart before they are realised in personal action (Matthew 15:18), enable us to place certain aspects of gun crime within Jesus' perspective on estrangement from God.

While reader response enables us to look afresh at the experience of people within the urban context, it does not effectively address the issues of power and justice that must be examined and applied to our social context if our interpretation of Scripture is to succeed in transforming and confronting systemic failure. In this respect it is necessary to deploy another strategy, namely ideological interpretation, and this is considered in the next chapter.

(The study questions are at the end of the next chapter and discuss both interpretive strategies.)

Chapter 9

Find the Power!
Ideological Interpretation

If you were raised to read the Bible spiritually then you may need some help to discover the issues of power within the Scriptures. At this point we turn to ideological interpretation. In order to comprehend the basics of this approach, we will begin by defining ideology and then exploring how it can be negatively used in interpreting the Bible.

Ideology

Essentially, an ideology is a system of ideas. Ideas rarely sit alone, but are often related to other ideas. For example, antiracism as a body of ideas is related to humanitarian ideas such as the right to live in peace without fear of brutality. When we talk about ideology as a system of ideas, we are interested in how these ideas are formed (where they came from?), challenged (is there another way of understanding this?), reproduced (how are they passed on?) and transformed (how are they changed?).[1]

Systems of ideas can be understood in two ways,[2] as either neutral or pejorative. The neutral understanding refers to ideology as a system of thought that forms part of everyday life. Here, the task of the one analysing ideology is to discover the systems of thoughts/beliefs operating within a given context. For example, the neutral deployment of ideology would examine the policies and ideas of Margaret Thatcher as a branch of contemporary politics. Similarly the business practice of the international restaurant chain McDonald's would be examined as a form of global capitalism. In short, the ideologically neutral approach identifies the 'isms' at work in a particular system of ideas.

In contrast, the pejorative (negative) meaning of ideology is concerned with the relationship between meaning and power, in particular how ideas preserve and sustain power relationships between people. It has been suggested that the pejorative interpretation is 'meaning in the service of power'.[3] From this perspective the policies and practices of Margaret Thatcher would be explored not just as being Conservative but through the lenses of Thatcherism – her particular view of the world. Likewise the McDonald's business chain would be analysed as a form either of global salvation or cultural imperialism, depending on one's politics.

Ideological critics of the Bible have adopted this second meaning. They look for systems of ideas in the Bible (ideology), examine how these ideas got there (the behind-the-text factor in interpretation) and how churches today interpret these passages (reader response). The aim of ideological interpretation is to ascertain who loses out and who gains from a particular interpretation. Put bluntly, how are unjust power relations retained through a particular interpretation of Scripture? Naturally, oppression is complex and the powerful and powerless are not mutually exclusive categories. Therefore, who really wins and loses from a particular reading is not always easy to ascertain.[4]

Interpreting Ideologically

As with reader response, ideological critics believe that every reader approaches the Bible from a particular standpoint, so the reader never engages with the text in a neutral or unbiased reading. For instance, during Apartheid in South Africa, both the whites and blacks claimed the Exodus story as their own. For the whites the Exodus narrative was a foreshadowing of their ancestors' journey out of persecution in Europe and into the promised land of Southern Africa. For blacks it was a paradigm (model) of how God was going to set them free from the political and economic bondage of Apartheid. Given the dangers of bias, ideological approaches to the text require a high degree of self-awareness and also a sensitivity towards the bias within the biblical text and the context of the reader. Greater awareness forms part of the checks and balances of reading a passage of Scripture ideologically.

How is ideological interpretation achieved? I want to outline three aspects of this approach. The first aspect requires a particular orientation towards the Scriptures. We need to be suspicious in the best sense of the word. This means that we approach a biblical passage believing that there are hidden power dynamics at work *within the text* that we need to decode. To find them, the reader has to read against the text, that is to consider who gains and who loses from the way the passage is presented and understood. For some time, feminist theologians have suggested that this is the best way of addressing male bias within the world of the Bible.[5]

In a similar vein, the urban socio-political reader has to approach the text in search of new insights into the power dynamics at play in Scripture. We have to reread the life of Jesus focusing on the power dynamics at work in his actions and message. Who does Jesus empower, and who does he push to the margins? Black theologians argue that Jesus' central ideology is that of liberation. Jesus aims to empower the 'little people' of his day, the infirm, morally corrupt and ethnically problematic. Liberation ideology has implications for both victimisers and victims within the rubric of systemic failure. It offers redemption for those involved in gun crime and gang violence and hope and restoration for those who have suffered. Within this scheme all are equally damaged by the failings of the system.

The second aspect requires us to identify and challenge what we deem to be problematic ideologies at work in Scripture. That is to say, we need to be aware of the ways in which passages can be read so as to maintain in the present context any unjust power relations evident in the text itself. There are glaringly obvious examples of this second concern in the warped ethnography of Genesis 9[6] and the alleged theological justification given for the genocide of the people of Canaan in the conquest narratives of Joshua.[7] Seeking out ideologies of power is often the most difficult area for traditionalists to venture into. This is because they suggest that the Bible is not unproblematic as it contains other conflicting or questionable ideas.

The third aspect is to explore how contemporary ideologies have had an impact on Christian interpretive practices. For example, postcolonial analysis would suggest that the limited prophetic activity of urban churches is in part due to the continuing hold of white colonial theology. Afrocentric analysis would nurture a suspicion towards interpretation and practice that fails to take ethnicity and identity seriously. In short, ideological analysis demands that the urban churches are honest and identify the ideological forces impacting their practice. Only then can the literal exorcism of individuals, systems and institutions deemed to limit the life-giving flow of the Gospel begin.

In summary, in the two preceding chapters, I have provided two approaches to interpretation that I believe go some way towards challenging the limitations of the spiritualised approaches of many urban churches. I am not suggesting that these are always superior, but instead they provide an alternative for those seeking to find what Scripture has to say to us. While reader response provides us with a good resource for addressing the spiritualised approach, ideological criticism enables us to look at the Bible and Christian tradition in a new way by looking at the power dynamics which are revealed by the interpretive process.

Study Questions
- In reference to reader-response interpretation, what experiences, personal or communal, impact on how you interpret Scripture?
- Can a more politically sensitive reader more easily draw out socio-political themes and practices from Scripture?
- Are there negative ideologies in Scripture? Can you cite examples?
- What do you consider to be the benefits and disadvantages of interpreting Scripture ideologically?

Chapter 10

When Doing Wrong
Makes Us Right

I hope that by now you will be wondering how these frameworks can be applied in a practical way in church settings. The purpose of this chapter is to illustrate how reader response and ideological interpretation can be utilised in preaching. I have reproduced a sermon I preached in Birmingham in April 2003 in response to issues of systemic failure in the city. Implicit within the sermon are interpretations based on reader response and ideological analyses of the passage.

Introduction

> **Exodus 1:15–21**
> [15] Then the king of Egypt said to the Hebrew midwives, one of whom was named Shiph'rah and the other Pu'ah,
> [16] 'When you serve as midwife to the Hebrew women, and see them upon the birthstool, if it is a son, you shall kill him; but if it is a daughter, she shall live.'
> [17] But the midwives feared God, and did not do as the king of Egypt commanded them, but let the male children live.
> [18] So the king of Egypt called the midwives, and said to them, 'Why have you done this, and let the male children live?'
> [19] The midwives said to Pharaoh, 'Because the Hebrew women are not like the Egyptian women; for they are vigorous and are delivered before the midwife comes to them.'
> [20] So God dealt well with the midwives; and the people multiplied and grew very strong.
> [21] And because the midwives feared God he gave them families.

My wife is, as I write, seven months pregnant with our first child. My recent introduction into the world of childbirth has nurtured an interest in the social and political dimensions of childbirth and the role played by British midwives. One of the benefits of living in a country with a welfare state and an interventionist social policy is that every pregnant woman is given free childrearing classes run by midwives at the local doctor's surgery. Midwifery in Britain has expanded beyond simply assisting in the birth process to providing technical antenatal and postnatal care through the delivery of classes and seminars.

On our first visit to the hospital for a scan the black African Caribbean midwife gave us a token which allowed us to get free pictures of the scan to take away. I offered to reimburse her for the expense, but she said to me, 'Hey, I have to take care of my own people (African Caribbean) because no one else will.' This is the only recorded subversive activity we have noticed during our time at the hospital. I think it would be fair to say that in terms of striking and militant political union engagement with the state, compared with miners and fire-fighters, midwives rank low on the list of radical or politically strident voices in contemporary British life!

This however was not the case in the Exodus narrative. Here, the midwives are presented as subversive agents challenging the genocidal actions of a ruthless dictator and an oppressive regime. Women are presented to us in the story as salvific figures, that is, instruments and representatives of God's salvation. What excites me here is that salvation is a social, political and physical act; saving male children who face complete extermination.

What intrigues me most about this passage in Exodus is that God sanctions the apparent wrongdoing of the midwives. For their disobedience, the midwives are not only protected by God but also rewarded – in this case they are given families of their own.

This morning I would like to reflect on this text and relate it to our own contemporary situation. I want to propose that when faced with conditions that threaten the life of our community, like the midwives we sometimes have to do wrong in order to make right. There are two themes within this text that are central to the concept of doing wrong to make right. These are *subversive piety* and *revolutionary collusion.*

Subversive Piety

A subversive piety is devotion to God that automatically pitches individuals against a bankrupt ruling order. It is faith that is engaged in changing the way things are. Christians fighting for Civil Rights and against Apartheid exhibited the essence of subversive piety. But there are degrees of subversion. Sometimes subversive piety involves disobedience or wrongdoing in order for good to occur. Far too often in Christian circles piety is associated with a *soft and gentle* expression of faith. But here in Exodus 1, piety is presented in a revolutionary way – the midwives' devotion to God is such that they refuse to go along with the dictates of the government. In other words they take part in civil disobedience. Fortunately for these women, they are protected by God and blessed, but this is not always the case for those who choose a subversive piety as a means of changing the social order for the good.

For example, Caribbean history is littered with tensions between doing the will of God and falling into line with unjust laws. The role of women as salvific intermediaries within this conflict is generally unrecorded, partly because of patriarchy or male bias in the recording of history. However, one account of radical piety involving 'saving children' that resonates (in a disturbing way) with the account of the midwives in the Exodus story is found in infant mortality rates during slavery in the Caribbean. After the abolition of the slave trade in the early part of the nineteenth century slave owners in the British Caribbean were forced to 'breed' their own slaves rather than simply import them.

In order to entice slave women to collude with this process they introduced a crude and early form of maternity leave from slave duties. Intriguingly, while maternity leave was in force, rather than going into decline, the infant mortality rate rose. These women chose to see their children die rather than being born into the genocidal conditions of slavery. Being an expectant parent I now realise the strength of character required, but I will never understand the psychological despair that it takes to make this kind of decision – to see your children die, rather than have them born into bondage. Significantly the high infant mortality rate in islands such as Jamaica is now cited as one of the contributors to the eventual economic failure of Caribbean slavery.

There is a need for subversive piety today, if not on this scale! Many of us need to examine our lives and see if there are places where we need to say no to the dictates of the system if obeying them indirectly lead to the destruction of our children. I know from my own work in education that there are policies and practices of Eurocentric education that I cannot adhere to because obedience would limit my capacity to work with black and other minority students.

We need to do all that we can to save our male children today, especially those who face potentially genocidal-like circumstances in our community. I am not trying to reinvent patriarchy because we know that there are also issues facing young black women. However, it is clear that today many of our young men face an existence where the cultural, social and political fabric of their society has been stripped away to the extent that a significant percentage are more likely to graduate from prison than university.

If this potential 'social death' faced by many young men is understood as a dynamic equivalent of the genocidal conditions of the Exodus narrative then we must ask ourselves, 'Where are the midwives at work today? Where are God's subversive actors redeeming, restoring and transforming the lives of the male children?'

Revolutionary Collusion

As well as a subversive piety being present within this narrative there is also what I want to call a revolutionary collusion. Revolutionary collusion is a tool of subversive piety – it is one way of getting the job done. Revolutionary collusion involves use of positions of power and privilege to liberate the oppressed. What I mean by this is that the midwives are on one level colluding with the State but have no intention of fulfilling its objectives. Instead they are disobedient to the State but faithful to God to ensure that the males are saved and God's plan proceeds.

Revolutionary collusion is not a new idea in black history or culture. From slavery to the present, there have been numerous black men and women who have used their position to secure the freedom of others. In Caribbean history there are records of slaves who lived and worked in the master's house who acted as lookouts while other slaves escaped to freedom.

There is now, more than at any other time in black history in Britain, a need for people in positions of influence whether on the street or in parliament to engage in revolutionary collusion. Many of us find ourselves in a place where we have relative privilege and power, but are we hearing God's voice and using our status to ensure that the unjust dictates of our employers and institutions work to save these facing a social death? I'm not telling anyone to go out and break the law, but what I am advocating is that revolutionary collusion encourages us to use our privilege to challenge injustice wherever it manifests itself whether in homes, communities, streets or schools. *We have to do wrong in order to make things right.*

Subversive piety and revolutionary collusion are not everyday Christian virtues found in daily readings of devotional books. And there may be some here today who find it disturbing contemplating this kind of behaviour. If I were to read against this text, I'd challenge aspects of what the midwives did. Surely they should have 'come clean' about their devotional wrongdoing? I mean, are these values that we want to pass on to our children?

Ethically, the Bible demands truth telling. Truth telling is a powerful antidote to the tricks and lies of evil forces in the world. By telling the truth we free ourselves from the falsehoods in and around us and are thus able to live as emancipated people. This is why Jesus said to his Jewish followers in John 8:32 'And you will know the truth, and the truth will make you free.' But, I don't feel good about reading against the text in this situation.

This is because I believe that the passage tells us something very important about the nature of ethics in this world. Ethics are not always a simple case of right v. wrong. Sometimes you have to make relative choices. What I mean by this is that most of life is full of grey areas and we, as Christian people have to do our best to negotiate them with honesty and integrity. It's like trying to do good work with tools that are imperfect or trying to eat a meal with hands that are dirty – eating your meal will be a messy business! What the Exodus narrative provides us with is a social context where ethical decisions must be made with a *relative* awareness. Sometimes you have to be disobedient in order to be liberating and revolutionary.

The Exodus passage tells me that under dangerous conditions where there is wrongdoing by the State, subversive piety and revolutionary collusion are necessary and valued in the struggle to save the oppressed. This view is not as problematic as it seems if we look into our own respective histories. Many white working-class, Continental African, South Asian and African Caribbean histories are littered with significant individuals and groups now celebrated for disobeying the oppressor in order to save the oppressed.

As Baptists we often celebrate the white Baptist missionaries who repeatedly broke the law to enable slaves to learn to read and write, and indirectly undermined the plantation system. Revolutionary outcomes are often based in subversive activity.

So where is our civil disobedience today? Where are we being wise as serpents but appearing as harmless as doves? Sometimes *we have to do wrong in order to make things right*.

Conclusion

As I mentioned earlier, we live in a time when many of our young men live in a world of social death. And what hurts me most is that many of them are completely unaware of it. They think that playing the fool, imitating rappers such as 50 Cent or So Solid Crew will somehow enable them to negotiate the structural disadvantages bound up with being poor, undereducated and from a minority ethnic community.

One of the major tasks that confronts us as a church positioned strategically in this place at this time is to act as the midwives did in the story. My mother raised me right, so I know that most of the women in this congregation have acted as the Hebrew midwives did at some time in their lives and that sadly, many of the men have never even thought about it.

If we are to have an impact on gun crime and gang violence, we can't keep on using the same old approaches. The circumstances demand that to be salvific figures like the midwives, we have to get to grips with a subversive piety and a revolutionary collusion. *We have to do wrong in order to make things right.*

Study Questions
- Were the midwives right to disobey Pharaoh's command to kill all the male children?
- Can God's love and power be present in subversive activity today? How?
- Are there examples in history you can cite where Christians have been civilly disobedient?
- How can people in positions of privilege and power use their status to promote justice?

SECTION 4

Action

Chapter 11

Act Now, Think Later

Towards a Prophetic Action Paradigm in Response to Gun Crime and Gang Violence

This final section consists of a presentation of the nature of action required from urban churches in response to analytical and biblical reflection on systemic failure. I want to show that a prophetic action is required that takes intervention seriously, has a holistic and liberating quality, is complex (di-unital) and is motivated by the Spirit of God.

Action

Action is integral to theology. All Christians at some time have heard the phrase 'walk the talk'. It describes the importance of living out your faith and not just talking about it. In other words, 'faith with works' (James 2:18). Action is important in this methodology because it ensures that doing theology is synonymous with social change; we explore the meaning of God in the world in order to set about changing the way things are.

Urban church action is often limited to witness and welfare. Witness action focuses on evangelism. Put simply, the measure of a church is how many people it can get through the church doors. Here, the community is changed as believers come to know Jesus Christ as their personal saviour. This strategy responds to the 'more believers, less crime' approach.

The welfare model recognises the importance of acting justly in the community beyond being a good neighbour and paying taxes. It engages in welfare projects designed to assist those in need. This is what I call the 'clean up the mess' approach.

Both these approaches fail to get to grips with the complexity of the theology required to respond to systemic failure. I want to articulate a *prophetic action* as a legitimate response to systemic failure.

Prophetic Action

The model of the biblical prophet inspires prophetic action. The prophetic is fundamentally an expression of the will of God revealing how things should be. It is also an ethical quest to restore human dignity and accountability and is always wedded to justice. We only need to read the lives of the biblical prophets to see these virtues held up as standards for prophetic performance. So what does it mean to talk about prophetic action in response to systemic failure? There are five features to this approach.

Interventionist

> The sleeping giant of black churches is set to awaken with a 'street pastors' initiative as church leaders prepare to hit Britain's inner cities.
>
> Organisers believe the clergy can have a real impact in diverting black youngsters away from guns and drugs.
>
> The move is set to be launched tomorrow, January 28, in the wake of the killings of teenagers Latisha Shakespeare and Charlene Ellis.
>
> The unleashing of the black churches' power in the community is the most significant step in tackling gun crime since the Birmingham murders on January 2.
>
> *The Voice*
> 27 January 2003

Prophetic action is first and foremost direct action. It seeks to get involved. Whether preventative or transformative it always seeks to be 'in the right place at the right time'. Intervention is built on the theological presupposition that the Christian faith must be salt (preserving goodness) as well as light (illuminating) in order to be the good news of the Gospel in the world today. The life and mission of Jesus sets the perfect example to those seeking to intervene in the present crisis over gun crime and gang violence. The essence of the incarnation reminds us that God intervened through Jesus in order to save the world. In response to systemic failure, the interventionist dimension of prophetic action demands that the Church is always involved in the quest for justice. It should never be considered a 'sleeping giant' on social ethics.[1] In other words, the urban Church should not be asking 'Should we be involved?', but, 'Where and how should we be involved?' The work of the Young Disciples Youth Development is a good example of intervention. This is a small voluntary sector group with the singular aim of reaching out to young black people, most of whom are involved in or affected by gang culture. The project engages in outreach work and weekly group sessions that address the social, cultural and political needs of young black people at risk. It offers training courses, education, sports and entertainment opportunities as an alternative to committing crime. In 2002 this group worked with over 500 young people in the Aston and Handsworth areas of Birmingham.[2]

Holistic
Prophetic action in response to systemic failure has to be holistic. By this I mean it needs to seek a complete and inter-related response. It needs to recognise that to speak the life-transforming goodness of God into situations blighted by gun crime and gang violence is a multifaceted task that must address every aspect of systemic failure. For example, we cannot ignore the impact of the domestic and global economic forces which have produced deprived communities who see drugs and violence as the only legitimate means of employment. There is always a danger that

those seeking to be prophetic will fail to see the multi-dimensionality of the problem.

The sterling and exemplary work of Street Pastors in London illustrates the importance of a holistic response.[3] The Street Pastors initiative was formed by churches in London who wanted to have a direct presence on the streets blighted by crime. It is a good example of interventionist action. It is liberating in that it seeks to work with the 'least of these', that is the drug dealers, gang members and sex industry workers in some of the most deprived urban areas of Britain. However, it also represents the challenges facing the prophetic in the British context. Street Pastors must seek to be connected in an *explicit* or *political* way to other groups working against the systems, institutions and structures that underpin systemic failure. What happens on the streets is fundamentally related to what occurs in homes, schools, employment agencies and government buildings in a particular locality. A prophetic approach would seek to connect all agencies, institutions and structures in a co-ordinated and multifaceted response to systemic failure.

Liberating

Worried mums are to stage a national march to protest at the rising tide of gun violence on Britain's streets.

Supporters from all over the country will descend on south London this Saturday for the Mothers Against Guns march.

During the event, which starts at Camberwell Green Square, south London, campaign chief Lucy Cope, 47, whose son Damien, 22, was murdered, will present a petition of more than 25,000 signatures to Downing Street demanding tougher sentences for gun offences.

She said: 'I implore any mother out there to join in this march. Please back this campaign and help stop the killings.'

The Voice
27 November 2002

Prophetic action is also liberating in that it is concerned with intervening on behalf of the 'least of these'. In Matthew 25 Jesus informs his followers that they really and truly serve God when they serve the least amongst people. In Christian theology, serving the least in a political sense means siding with those who have been marginalised and brutalised by the current system. This approach is exemplified in the work of Mothers Against Guns (MAG).[4] Formed by mothers who have lost offspring to gun crime, they are interventionists in that they seek to intervene on behalf of victims' families, who are often made voiceless within the criminal justice system. They are also holistic in that they recognise that gun crime is related to wholesale social failure in urban Britain. But most significantly they are liberating in that they seek to give a voice to the voiceless victims who are often left to suffer alone. MAG's support work exemplifies what it means to serve 'the least'.

However, within the urban context traditional distinctions made between victim and victimiser are not always clear cut. Take for example the position of gang members – in many cases their life histories suggest that they are both victim and victimiser. Therefore, the liberating task of prophetic action is critical in helping us to recognise that the vile consequences of oppression brutalise all of us in some way, and some more than others.

Di-unital

Because prophetic action is holistic and liberating it also seeks to be di-unital.[5] Di-unital action, rather than seeing the world in black and white, recognises grey areas. This perspective is sometimes called a both/and action rather than an either/or action.

Whereas the holistic impulse seeks to interconnect, di-unitalism appreciates tensions and differences. Too often, prophetic action is presented as an either/or option for black communities. For instance, there have been times when churches have decided that they will either pray for change or take social action unaware that these two strategies are not mutually exclusive. Di-unital thought recognises that when addressing any issue related to systemic failure our response must recognise tensions and seek to be 'both/and' rather than 'either/or'.

Spiritual

Prophetic action is also spiritual on two levels. The first level recognises that prophetic action, to be truly effective, must be directed by the Spirit of God. To talk of the Spirit of God is not wishy-washy or superfluous – we are referring to God's agent of change in the world today. The Spirit is not exclusive to the urban Church or satellite organisations, as the Spirit has to accomplish God's mission in the world today. The Spirit is moving despite the limitations of the urban Church (praise God!) and is found wherever people are doing the work and will of God.[6] In response to systemic failure we might say that the Spirit of God is found where men and women are working to address the causes and consequences of systemic failure in a manner that restores dignity, accountability and justice.

For example, while not professing to be a religious organisation, Young Disciples Youth Development in Aston, Birmingham is clearly guided by the Spirit. The Young Disciples is interventionist, in that former gang members founded it to reach out to and offer hope to current members. It is also liberating in that it seeks to empower those who find themselves on the wrong side of the law and challenge socially-acceptable morality. It is also holistic in that it recognises that the social exclusion experienced by many black urban youths is the product of multiple failings.[7]

On another level within the dimension of prophetic action the Spirit is a source of regenerative power. The Spirit is concerned with concrete change; that is, making war against the powers of non-being and evil, breaking down strongholds and ushering in a new reality. The Spirit ensures that 'greater works' (John 14:12) will be accomplished than in the time of Jesus. The Spirit of God is capable of doing what cannot naturally be achieved by human might because some of the battles we face are not carnal or physical but spiritual (2 Corinthians 10:4). To harness the power of the Spirit of God is fundamental to prophetic action for without the Spirit 'it is nothing'.

In Caribbean culture the old folks talk of 'duppy conquering'. Those familiar with Caribbean folklore will know that this phrase refers to getting rid of the problematic spiritual forces that inhibit human life (the 'duppy' is a spirit of the deceased). This is why the reggae legend Bob Marley sings of 'Duppy Conquering' as an act of liberation and redemption in one of his songs. The Spirit of God is a 'duppy conqueror'. The Spirit challenges the forces of non-being by providing those in pursuit of the will of God with the tools to see the way things really should be. This is because the Spirit brings truth and truth destabilises falsehood, enables us to see the way things should be and makes space for us to construct a new way of living and being.

In summary, in this chapter I have suggested the type of action that should arise from the analysis and theological reflection in which the urban Church is encouraged to engage in prophetic action. Prophetic action is multilayered; it intervenes, it is holistic, and it is di-unital. It focuses on the marginalised (liberative) and smashes icons, in that it seeks to conqueror the forces of non-being through the power of the Spirit.

Study Questions

- How would you classify the way your church acts: witness, welfare or prophetic?
- What are the benefits and dangers of intervention?
- Should intervention always be on behalf of 'the least of these'?
- Can prophetic action be conducted without the Spirit of God? What does the Spirit offer?
- Can you think of interventionist groups in your locality or at national level? What distinguishes their approach? Which aspects would you choose to emulate?

Conclusion

God and All the Gangs

As mentioned in the introduction, this book was written in response to the Birmingham New Year shootings in 2003. My aim has been to provide tools that urban churches might make use of as they attempt to engage with systemic failure (the plethora of social issues of which gun crime and gang violence are a small part). Serious limitations in thinking were exhibited in a series of meetings organised by the Council of Black-led Churches in Birmingham in response to the shootings. As one of the few theologically trained participants, I wanted to make a constructive and lasting contribution by putting pen to paper.

If urban churches are prepared to take seriously engagement with and analysis of the social world as a starting-point for theological inquiry then dialogue between the Church and community will be enhanced and barriers broken down between the two. There are now churches emerging in London, Birmingham and Manchester with this specific remit – to seek and save gang members.

However, outreach to gang members is thwarted with difficulties too numerous to explore in this toolkit. In order to avoid some of the potential pitfalls, I have suggested that serious analysis must take place. We can only get to the analysis as urban churches embrace a critical intellectualism that fosters sound reason, rigorous engagement and divine wisdom. Being a religious–cultural scholar, I have proposed specific religious–

cultural analytical tools. Naturally, these are limited but offer insight into some of the basic issues at hand.

I believe that underpinning the present crisis is a long-term problem – the inability to confront and transform the colonial legacy inside and outside urban churches. In this new domestic colony, new forms of economic, political and cultural oppression continue to devastate urban communities. We can't discuss systemic failure without exploring the colonising processes evident in schooling, policing and municipal government. I am also convinced that identity politics need to be discussed and explored in our quest to regenerate the lives and minds of black youths who have left school with little appreciation of their cultural heritage apart from steel bands and limbo dancing. To this end, aspects of Afrocentricity are fundamental to re-visioning history, community and solidarity amongst black urban people.

However, not everyone who lives in the urban context is black, Asian or Chinese. There has always been a sizable and sometimes majority white community in the inner city. In some instances gentrification has seen a new white middle class carve out space in what were once perceived as no-go areas. I believe that balanced and politicised members of the white community also have a role to play in the response to systemic failure. After the shootings in January 2003 white priests, community workers and media journalists offered their skills in service to the community. From these white activists black urban folk demand a critical whiteness – a political outlook that will enable them to really engage in the struggle against systemic failure for the long haul and with other ethnic groups.

Many of the battles fought over the interpretation of events after the shootings took place in the media. The media is the new front line. It is the place where black bodies are electronically brutalised and digitally lynched. Cultural analysis can help us make sense of and challenge images but it must also be used to nurture healthy suspicion amongst urban communities towards everything that is presented as 'authentic black culture'.

The way we use the Bible can either save or hinder the battle to save those caught up in gun crime and gang violence. It can save if it is read in the light of social analysis, but it will continue to be a limited resource if we persist in believing that the only way the Spirit can speak to us is through interpretations that are 'spiritualised'. That is to say, its power is limited if we ignore the concrete socio-political issues and power dynamics at play in Scripture, and how they contribute to a re-appraisal of understanding of the nature of the mission of the Church in the world today.

I believe that only socio-politically informed urban church readers/activists, those able to engage in a meaningful dialogue between the political world of Scripture and ours today, offer a route out of the current 'cul-de-sac' hermeneutics on offer in most black urban churches on Sundays.

However, faith without works does not count for much (James 2:20), so we need to be prepared to act and act quickly to make an impression. I have proposed a 'prophetic action' as the way in which experience, analysis and biblical reflection converge in response to systemic failure. We need action that is immediate and targeted. Furthermore, because systemic failure is complex and layered, our action must be multilayered, addressing the numerous areas of failure and oppression. Tragically, many of the areas in which we need to act are within urban communities themselves. If we cannot find ways of working in a meaningful way with the police to provide criminal intelligence or confront and dismiss those responsible for mismanagement of local agencies, then our action is severely weakened. The ability to self-criticise is a good indicator of a healthy and balanced diagnosis of and prognosis for the situation.

In reality, action is not the last part of the equation, but should accompany all aspects of our analysis. For analysis, reflection and action will show that systemic failure does not only impact the young people bearing arms. Prophetic action must ultimately address the 'gangs' in local and national government responsible for failed policies, the 'gangs' in the media responsible for neocolonial journalism and visual culture. Finally, prophetic action must also address the 'gangs' in the churches that have allowed themselves to be bought out, sold out and scared out of being a prophetic witness to the gangs on the streets.

Notes

Introduction: Sold Out, Bought Out, Scared Out

1. When I mention the urban Church I refer to Christian congregations in the urban context. African and African Caribbean worshippers dominate many urban contexts and churches. Therefore, I refer mainly (but not exclusively) to these black majority congregations. 'Black urban churches' will be used to designate churches or denominations that are nearly 100 per cent black. Please note that the notion of blackness is not used as a monolith. 'Black' is used in a postmodern sense that recognises a lived tension of difference and sameness. Finally, in black Christian traditions in Britain, 'church' has always been a fluid reality. Black people, have formal and informal ways of worshipping and communing with each other and with God. This is why black Christians often use the phrase 'we had church' to describe any occasion where there was an experience of God amongst believers. Thus 'church' can occur literally anywhere.
2. Alan Travis, 'Summit over 35% Gun Crime Rise', *Guardian*, 10 January 2003. See www.guardian.co.uk/uk__news/story/0,3604,872027,00.html
3. When I refer to gun crime and gang violence I refer specifically to the rise in incidents of shootings, murders and gang-related crime such as drug dealing, petty crime and general social disorder.
4. Hugh Muir, 'Criminal Captains of Commerce', *Guardian*, 20 June 2003. See www.guardian.co.uk/uk__news/story/0,3604,981230,00.html
5. Stephen Moore, *Investigating Crime and Deviance*, HarperCollins, 1996, p. 242ff.
6. Muir, 'Criminal Captains of Commerce'.
7. I present these as generalisations to mark the boundaries of particular perspectives but I recognise that these camps are more complex and fluid than is often thought.
8. Andrew Perriman (ed.), *Faith, Health and Prosperity: A Report on 'Word of Faith' and 'Positive Confession' Theologies by THE Evangelical Alliance (UK) Commission on Unity and Truth among Evangelicals*, Paternoster Press, 2003, p. xvii.
9. Kenneth Leech, *Struggle in Babylon: Racism in the Cities and Churches of Britain*, Sheldon Press, 1988.
10. Ron Ramdin, *The Making of the Black Working Class in Britain*, Gower Publishing Company, 1988, p. 187ff.
11. Robert Beckford, *Jesus is Dread: Black Theology and Black Culture in Britain*, Darton, Longman and Todd, 1998; *God of the Rahtid: Redeeming Rage*, Darton, Longman and Todd, 2001.
12. Paul Gilroy, *Small Acts: Thoughts on the Politics of Black Cultures*, Serpent's Tail, 1993. See also Lola Young, *Fear of the Dark: 'Race', Gender and Sexuality in the Cinema*, Routledge, 1996.

Chapter 1: Urban Style: Towards a Relevant Theological Method

1. For the comic and film character 'Superman', kryptonite is a cosmic material that, upon contact with him, turns him into a mere mortal.
2. Emmanuel Y. Lartey, *In Living Colour: An Intercultural Approach to Pastoral Care and Counselling*, Cassell, 1997, p. 94ff.
3. Leonardo and Clodovis Boff, *Introducing Liberation Theology*, Burns and Oates, 1987, p. 22ff.
4. Martin Bright, 'One in 10 Jamaican Fliers Is a Drug Mule', *Observer*, 23 February 2003. See also Jeevan Vasgar 'East European Gunrunners Boost UK Gang Weaponry', *Guardian*, 2 July 2003.
5. Iain MacRobert, *Black Pentecostalism: Its Origins and Functions*, PhD thesis, University of Birmingham, 1989.
6. Cornel West, *Prophesy Deliverance! An Afro-American Revolutionary Christianity*, Westminster Press, 1982, p. 47ff.
7. James H. Cone, *God of the Oppressed*, HarperCollins, 1975, pp. 39–108.
8. See my evaluation of this research in Robert Beckford, *Dread and Pentecostal: A Political Theology for the Black Church in Britain*, SPCK, 2000.

Chapter 2: Are You Listening? Experience As Our Starting-Point

1. R. S. Sugirtharajah (ed.), *Voices from the Margin: Interpreting the Bible in the Third World*, SPCK, 1991.
2. For example, Stuart Hall talks of the ideological negotiation of resistance in the Caribbean among slave communities. Stuart Hall, 'Religious Ideologies and Social Movements in Jamaica' in Robert Bocock and Kenneth Thompson (eds) *Religion and Ideology*, Manchester University Press, 1985.
3. See John Solomos and Les Back, *Racism and Society*, Macmillan Press, 1996, p. 202ff.
4. Valentina Alexander calls this approach, 'passive radicalism'. See Valentina Alexander, *Breaking Every Fetter? To What Extent Has the Black-led Church in Britain Developed a Theology of Liberation?*, PhD thesis, University of Warwick, 1997.
5. This point is made in a study by Nicole Rodriguez Toulis, *Believing Identity: Pentecostalism and the Mediation of Jamaican Ethnicity and Gender in England*, Berg, 1997, p. 165ff.
6. Emilie M. Townes (ed.) *Embracing the Spirit: Womanist Perspectives on Hope, Salvation and Transformation*, Orbis, 1997.
7. Robert E. Hood, *Must God Remain Greek?: Afro-Cultures and God Talk*, Fortress Press, 1990, p. 43ff.
8. Paul Gilroy, *The Black Atlantic: Modernity and Double Consciousness*, Verso, 1992.
9. Cornel West, *Race Matters*, Beacon Press, 1993.
10. See James W. Messerschmidt, *Crime As Structured Action: Gender, Race, Class and Crime in the Making*, Sage, 1997.
11. Muir, 'Criminal Captains of Commerce'.

Chapter 3: Old and New Colonies: The Continued Impact of Colonialism

1. A. Sivanandan, *A Different Hunger: Writings on Black Resistance*, Pluto Press, 1982.
2. R. S. Sugirtharajah, *Postcolonial Criticism and Biblical Interpretation*, Oxford University Press, 2002.
3. 'Empire: How Britain Made the Modern World', Channel 4, 2003.
4. Winston James and Clive Harris, *Inside Babylon: The Caribbean Diaspora in Britain*, Verso, 1993, ch. 1.
5. Stephen Small, *Racialised Barriers: The Black Experience in the United States and England in the 1980s*, Routledge, 1994, p. 110ff.
6. Frantz Fanon, *Black Skin, White Masks*, Pluto Press, 1991.
7. Patricia Hill Collins, *Black Feminist Thought: Knowledge, Power and the Politics of Empowerment*, Routledge, 1990. See her chapter on Eurocentric knowledge validation.
8. Barnor Hesse (ed.) *Unsettled Multiculturalism: Diasporas, Entanglements, Transcriptions*, Zed Books, 2000, ch. 1.
9. Amina Mama, *Beyond the Mask: Race, Gender and Subjectivity*, Routledge, 1995, pp. 47–8.
10. Peter Fryer, *Staying Power*, Gower Press, 1988, p. 133ff.
11. Ibid.
12. Robert E. Hood, *Begrimed and Black: Christian Traditions on Black and Blackness*, Fortress Press, 1994, pp. 1–23.
13. Kenan Malik, *The Meaning of Race: Race, History and Culture in Western Society*, Macmillan Press, 1996.
14. See Paul Oliver (ed.) *Black Music in Britain: Essays on the Afro-Asian Contribution to Popular Music*, Open University Press, 1990, p. 102ff.
15. Alexander, *Breaking Every Fetter?*
16. Beckford, *Dread and Pentecostal*.
17. Kortright Davis, *Emancipation Still Commin': Explorations in Caribbean Emancipatory Theology*, Orbis, 1990.
18. Horace Campbell, *From Rasta to Resistance: From Marcus Garvey to Walter Rodney*. London, Hancib Publications, 1985.
19. Hood, *Must God Remain Greek?*
20. Ibid.
21. Beckford, *Jesus is Dread*.

Chapter 4: More than Just a Bass Line: Cultural Analysis

1. Fiachra Gibbons, 'Minister Labelled Racist After Attack on Rap "Idiots" ', *Guardian*, 6 January 2003. See www.guardian.co.uk/uk_news/story/0,3604,869390,00.html
2. This is the view presented by cultural critic Professor Michael Eric Dyson in 'Ebony Towers: The Rise of the Black Intelligentsia' BBC4, January 2003.
3. Glenn Jordan and Chris Weedon (eds) *Cultural Politics: Class, Gender, Race and the Postmodern World*, Oxford University Press, 1995, pp. 6–10.
4. Dick Hebdige, *Cut 'N' Mix: Culture, Identity and Caribbean Music*, Routledge, 1987.
5. Les Back, *New Ethnicities and Urban Culture*, UCL Press, 1996.

6. Michael Eric Dyson, 'Ebony Towers'.

7. Michael Eric Dyson, *Holler If You Hear Me: Searching for Tupac Shakur*, Basic Cevitas Books, 2001.

8. Black British academic, Tony Sewell, expresses this view. See Gaby Hinsliff and Martin Bright, 'Black Youth Culture Blamed as Pupils Fail', *Observer*, 20 August 2000. See www.observer.guardian.co.uk/uk__news/story/ 0,6903,356543,00.html

Chapter 5: The Place of Blackness: Afrocentric Analysis

1. Paul Gilroy, *Against Race: Imagining Political Culture Beyond the Color Line*, Harvard University Press, 2000.

2. Kobena Mercer, *Welcome to the Jungle: New Positions in Black Cultural Studies*, Routledge, 1990.

3. Molefi Kete Asante, *Afrocentricity*, Africa World Press, 1988.

4. Edward Kamau Brathwaite, *Folk Cultures of the Slaves in Jamaica*, New Beacon Books, 1981.

5. Stephen Howe, *Afrocentrism: Mythical Pasts and Imagined Homes*, Verso, 1998, p. 1.

6. Paul Gilroy, *Small Acts*.

7. M. Karenga, *Introduction to Black Studies*, second edition, The University of Sankore Press, 1993, p. 34.

8. See the criticism of Afrocentrism in Stephen Howe, *Afrocentrism*.

9. C. Sanders (ed.), *Living the Intersection: Womanism and Afrocentrism in Theology*, Fortress Press, 1995, p. 158.

10. Barbara Summers, *Black and Beautiful*, HarperCollins, 2001.

11. Davis, *Emancipation Still Commin'*.

12. Maxine Howell-Baker and Tonya Bolton, *Am I My Brother's / Sister's Keeper? Black Majority Churches and Development*, Christian Aid, 2003.

13. Randall Bailey, 'Beyond Identification: The Use of Africans in Old Testament Poetry and Narratives', in Cain Hope Felder (ed.), *Stony the Road We Trod: African American Biblical Interpretation*, Fortress Press, 1991.

14. Ibid., p. 181.

Chapter 6: What Does It Mean to Be White? Understanding Whiteness in the Urban Context

1. Steven Morris, 'Coroner in race row at shooting inquest', *Guardian*, 10 January 2003. See www.guardian.co.uk/uk__news/story/0,3604,871798,00.html

2. Frantz Fanon, *The Wretched of the Earth*, Penguin, 1990.

3. I have tried to explore this issue for black British people in *God of the Rahtid*.

4. See the discussion on the contemporary realities of multicultural Britain and the problems for African Caribbean and African people, 'The Truth of Multiculturalism' by Sunder Katwala in the *Observer*, 25 November 2001 at www.observer.guardian.co.uk/race/story/0,11255,605337,00.html

5. See 'UN set to tackle Britain on racism' by Martin Bright, *Observer*, 13 August 2000. See www.observer.guardian.co.uk/uk__news/story/0,6903,353751, 00.html

6. See Birgit Brander et al., *Making and Unmaking of Whiteness*, Duke University Press, 2001, introduction.

7. Vron Ware and Les Back, *Out of Whiteness: Color, Politics and Culture*, The University of Chicago Press, 2002.
8. See the study on the pain of entry into whiteness by Thandeka, *Learning to be White*, Continuum, 2001.

Chapter 7: The Politics of Interpretation

1. N. Holland, 'Unity Identity Text Self', *PMLA* 1975, 90:813–22, 124.
2. Davis, *Emancipation Still Commin'*.
3. Kelly Brown Douglas, *The Black Christ*, Orbis, 1994.
4. S. Fish, *Surprised by Sin: The Reader in* Paradise Lost, second edition, University of California Press, 1971. See also *Is There a Text in This Class? The Authority of Interpretative Communities*, Harvard University Press, 1980.
5. Fish, *Is There a Text in This Class?*
6. Severio Croatto, *Biblical Hermeneutics: Towards a Theory of Reading As the Production of Meaning.* Orbis, 1987, p. 5ff.
7. Ibid., p. 6.
8. Ibid., p. 7.
9. Felder, *Stony the Road We Trod*.
10. Randall Bailey, 'They're Nothing But Incestuous Bastards: The Polemical Use of Sex and Sexuality in the Hebrew Canon Narratives', in Fernando F. Segovia and Mary Ann Tolbert (eds), *Reading From This Place: Social Location and Biblical Interpretation in the United States*, Fortress Press, 1995.

Chapter 8: Me, My Text and I: Reader Response Interpretation

1. For a good discussion of contemporary debates see Elizabeth A. Castelli (ed.), The Bible and Culture Collective, *The Postmodern Bible: The Bible and Culture Collective*, Yale University Press, 1997.
2. MacRobert, *Black Pentecostalism*.
3. Bailey, 'They're Nothing But Incestuous Bastards'.

Chapter 9: *Find* the Power! Ideological Interpretation

1. Castelli, *The Postmodern Bible*, p. 272.
2. John B. Thompson, *Ideology and Modern Culture*, Polity Press, 1992, pp. 5–7.
3. Ibid., p. 7.
4. M. Volf, *Exclusion and Embrace: A Theological Exploration of Identity, Otherness and Reconciliation*, Abingdon Press, 1996, pp. 101–5.
5. Ann Loades, *Feminist Theology: A Reader*, SPCK, 1990.
6. See Cain Hope Felder's analysis of the ancient ethnography at work here in Felder, *Stony the Road We Trod*.
7. See Robert Warrior's classic analysis from an American Indian perspective in 'Canaanites, Cowboys and Indians: Deliverance, Conquest and Liberation Theology Today', *Christianity and Crisis* 29:261–56

Chapter 11: Act Now, Think Later

1. *The Voice*, 27 January 2003.
2. Dr Liz Hoggarth and David Wright, 'Young Disciples Research and Evaluation Report', Crime Concern Trust, July 2003.
3. *The Voice*, 27 January 2003.
4. *The Voice*, 27 November 2002.

5. For further discussion see Garth Baker-Fletcher and Karen Baker-Fletcher, *My Sister, My Brother: Womanist and Xodus God-Talk*, Orbis, 1997. p. 16ff.
6. Veli-Matti Karkkainen, *Pneumatology: The Holy Spirit in Ecumenical, International and Contextual Perspective*, Baker Academic, 2002, p. 30ff.
7. Conversation with Mark Edwards of Young Disciples, 5 July 2003.